PRAISE FOR *NEVER CAUGHT,* *THE STORY OF ONA JUDGE*

A 2019 NEW YORK PUBLIC LIBRARY BEST BOOK FOR KIDS
AN *SLJ* BEST BOOK OF 2019

★ "The accessible narrative, clear context, and intricately recorded details of the lives of the enslaved provide much-needed understanding of the complexities and contradictions of the country's founding. Necessary." —*KIRKUS REVIEWS,* STARRED REVIEW

★ "In this young readers' edition of her adult work *Never Caught,* Dunbar ably surmounts the challenge of building a gripping, coherent narrative from oblique references and interviews with elderly Ona Judge Staines, while steadily keeping the focus on Judge rather than her high-profile owners." —*BCCB,* STARRED REVIEW

★ "This well-written story has been skillfully reconstructed from the sparse historical record available and delicately adapted for middle schoolers. Dunbar and van Cleve effectively and consistently convey the realities of being enslaved—and invite readers to empathize with Judge. . . . A brilliant work of U.S. history. Recommended for all collections." —*SLJ,* STARRED REVIEW

ALSO BY ERICA ARMSTRONG DUNBAR

*She Came to Slay: The Life and Times
of Harriet Tubman*

*A Fragile Freedom: African American Women
and Emancipation in the Antebellum City*

AND BY KATHLEEN VAN CLEVE

Drizzle

YOUNG READERS EDITION

NEVER CAUGHT,

THE STORY OF ONA JUDGE

GEORGE AND MARTHA WASHINGTON'S
COURAGEOUS SLAVE WHO DARED TO RUN AWAY

By ERICA ARMSTRONG DUNBAR
and KATHLEEN VAN CLEVE

Aladdin
New York London Toronto Sydney New Delhi

ALADDIN

An imprint of Simon & Schuster Children's Publishing Division
1230 Avenue of the Americas, New York, New York 10020
First Aladdin paperback edition May 2020
Text copyright © 2017, 2019 by Erica Armstrong Dunbar
This young readers edition is adapted from *Never Caught* by Erica Armstrong Dunbar, published in 2017 by 37 Ink/Atria Books.
Cover and map illustration copyright © 2019 by Shadra Strickland
Photographs and transcription on pages 235–239: "Washington's Runaway Slave," *Granite Freeman*, May 22, 1845. Courtesy of the New Hampshire Historical Society.
Also available in an Aladdin hardcover edition.

For information about special discounts for bulk purchases, please contact Simon & Schuster Special Sales at 1-866-506-1949 or business@simonandschuster.com.
The Simon & Schuster Speakers Bureau can bring authors to your live event.
For more information or to book an event contact the Simon & Schuster Speakers Bureau at 1-866-248-3049 or visit our website at www.simonspeakers.com.
Cover designed by Laura Lyn DiSiena and Angela Navarra
Interior designed by Mike Rosamilia
The text of this book was set in Bembo Std.
Manufactured in the United States of America 1120 OFF
4 6 8 10 9 7 5
The Library of Congress has cataloged the hardcover edition as follows:
Names: Dunbar, Erica Armstrong, author.
Title: Never Caught, the story of Ona Judge : George and Martha Washington's courageous slave who dared to run away / by Erica Armstrong Dunbar and Kathleen Van Cleve.
Description: Young readers edition. | New York : Aladdin, [2019] | Includes bibliographical references and index. | Audience: Ages 9-13.
Identifiers: LCCN 2018043941 (print) | LCCN 2018044888 (eBook) | ISBN 9781534416192 (eBook) | ISBN 9781534416178 (hc)
Subjects: LCSH: Judge, Oney—Juvenile literature. | Slaves—United States—Biography—Juvenile literature. | Fugitive slaves—United States—Biography—Juvenile literature. | African American women—Biography—Juvenile literature. | Washington, George, 1732-1799—Relations with slaves—Juvenile literature. | Washington, Martha, 1731-1802—Relations with slaves—Juvenile literature. | Slavery—Pennsylvania—Philadelphia—History—18th century—Juvenile literature.
Classification: LCC E444 (eBook) | LCC E444 .D86 2019 (print) | DDC 306.3/62092 [B]—dc23
LC record available at https://lccn.loc.gov/2018043941
ISBN 9781534416185 (pbk)

For my favorite young and young adult readers:
Leah Grace Armstrong and Christian Andrew Dunbar
—E. A. D.

And for my favorite readers, young and old:
Emory, Jackson, and Emerson Van Cleve
—K. V. C.

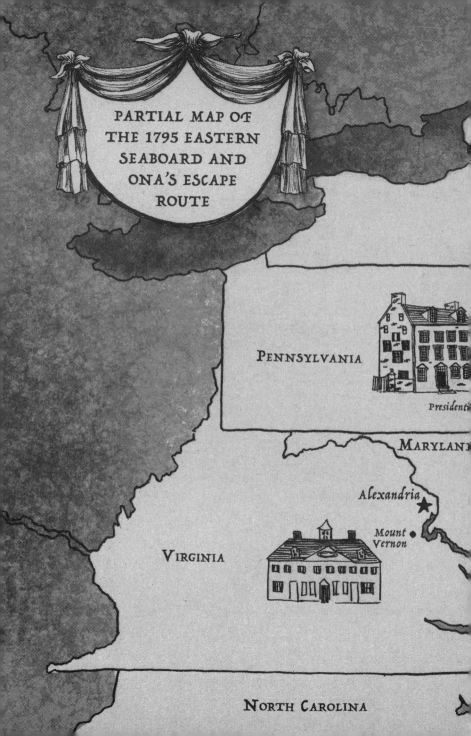

PARTIAL MAP OF THE 1795 EASTERN SEABOARD AND ONA'S ESCAPE ROUTE

PENNSYLVANIA

President

MARYLAND

Alexandria

Mount Vernon

VIRGINIA

NORTH CAROLINA

MASSACHUSETTS*

VERMONT

NEW
HAMPSHIRE
Portsmouth ★

NEW YORK

MASSACHUSETTS*

CONNECTICUT

RHODE
ISLAND

Philadelphia
sion ● ★

NEW
JERSEY

DELAWARE

Delaware Bay

ATLANTIC OCEAN

N

W   E

S

*In 1795, Massachusetts also included
territory that is in present-day Maine.

CONTENTS

AUTHOR'S NOTE

Dear Reader,

I am delighted that your eyes have met these words! You are about to encounter a story of bravery and heroism that will make you think differently about everything you have learned regarding American history. This is a book about a young woman who, in the face of great difficulty, did what no one imagined possible. You are about to meet Ona Judge, a young enslaved woman who was the human property of two of the most well-known people in the history of the United States. Ona was enslaved by George and Martha Washington.

I use the word "enslaved" a lot throughout this book. It is a word that reminds us that millions of people were brought to America against their will from Africa and, later, the Caribbean. These people were "enslaved." That is, they were forced to become slaves. It was an act that was placed upon them by others. When you look up the word "slave" in the dictionary, it says the following: "a person who is the legal property of another and is forced to obey them." To be a slave in the United States usually meant that you would spend your entire life in bondage. Enslaved men and women were not allowed to legally marry. (But they did fall in love and pick their own husbands and wives.) It was illegal to teach southern slaves how to read or write, and for hundreds of years, millions of black people were sold away from their families, beaten, whipped, and sometimes killed.

There's no way to ease into the topic of American slavery. Slavery was brutal. Slavery was immoral. Slavery was an unjust system that kept black people at the bottom of society's social ladder. While all of this can be uncomfortable to read about and discuss, we must do so. If we want to build a better present and future, we must recognize and understand the problems of the past. Young readers are exactly the people who need to know this history. This book is for readers who are in elementary and middle school, and it will prepare them for history in high school and beyond. I also wrote this book for teachers. Teachers are champions! It is my wish that more historians will write for young readers so that teachers can have a variety of books for their classrooms.

Ona's story tells us what it was like to be enslaved when this nation was first founded. Her life begins as a slave on the Washingtons' Mount Vernon estate in Virginia and ends with her living as a free woman in New Hampshire. Ona lived a long life and experienced many tragedies. But she also found love and joy in the midst of great despair.

Ona was a survivor.

It gives me great pride to introduce Ona Maria Judge to a world of younger readers. I hope that everyone who reads these pages will find strength in Ona's courage.

Erica Armstrong Dunbar

Please note: There were many documents used in the writing of this book. These documents, called primary sources, often include words that are spelled incorrectly and phrases that are grammatically incorrect. I have decided to alter some of the quotes so that they are easier to read.

TIME LINE

June 2, 1731	Martha Washington is born in Virginia.
February 22, 1732	George Washington is born in Virginia.
circa 1738	Betty (Ona's mother) is born.
circa 1757	Austin (Ona's half brother) is born in Virginia.
January 6, 1759	George and Martha Washington are married at Mount Vernon.
circa 1769	Tom Davis (Ona's half brother) is born at Mount Vernon.
circa 1771	Betty Davis (Ona's half sister) is born at Mount Vernon.
circa 1773–74	Ona Judge is born at Mount Vernon.
September–October 1774	First Continental Congress meets in Philadelphia.

April 19, 1775	The Battles of Lexington and Concord (first battles of the American Revolution) occur.
May 1775	Second Continental Congress meets in Philadelphia.
June 15, 1775	General George Washington is appointed commander in chief of the Continental Army.
July 1776	Declaration of Independence is created in Philadelphia.
circa 1780	Philadelphia (Ona's half sister) is born at Mount Vernon.
March 1, 1780	Gradual Abolition Act is passed in Pennsylvania.
September 3, 1783	Treaty of Paris is signed and ratified, ending the war between Great Britain and America and recognizing American independence.
1783–1784	Ona is called up to the mansion house to work.
May–September 1787	Constitutional Convention is held in Philadelphia.
April 30, 1789	George Washington is inaugurated in New York as the first president of the United States of America.

May 1789	Ona accompanies Martha Washington to New York.
November 1790	Ona accompanies the Washingtons to Philadelphia.
February 1793	Congress enacts the Fugitive Slave Law.
December 1794	Austin dies in Harford, Maryland.
January 1795	Betty (Ona's mother) dies at Mount Vernon.
March 1796	Eliza Parke Custis marries Thomas Law.
May 21, 1796	Ona Judge escapes from Philadelphia.
Fall 1796	Joseph Whipple tries to convince Ona to return to the Washingtons.
January 1797	Ona marries Jack Staines in New Hampshire.
March 1797	George Washington steps down from office.
circa 1798	Ona gives birth to Eliza Staines.
Fall 1799	Burwell Bassett Jr. tries to kidnap Ona.
December 1799	George Washington dies at Mount Vernon.
circa 1800	Ona gives birth to William Staines.

circa 1802	Ona gives birth to Nancy Staines.
May 1802	Martha Washington dies at Mount Vernon.
1803	Jack Staines dies.
June 1807	Philadelphia (Ona's half sister) is emancipated.
May 1845	The interview with Ona appears in the *Granite Freeman*.
January 1847	The interview with Ona appears in the *Liberator*.
February 25, 1848	Ona Maria Judge Staines dies in Greenland, New Hampshire.

THE ESCAPE

ONA MARIA JUDGE, A SLAVE SINCE BIRTH TO GEORGE AND Martha Washington, didn't typically serve dinner to her owners. It was the one time of day when she didn't have to worry whether she was quiet enough or helpful enough or invisible enough; the kitchen staff dealt with meals, not her. Usually Ona was upstairs or outside or in the back kitchen, treasuring her moments away from her 24/7 life of slavery.

On Saturday, May 21, 1796, this changes. Watching the dining room from the hallway of the President's House in Philadelphia, Ona's eyes flit back and forth between George and Martha, perhaps eating their salt fish, drinking their wine, discussing things she can't hear. It is time. Now or never: she has made a decision, and now the only question is whether she will have the guts to go through with it.

Escape.

She takes a deep breath. A force inside her compels her to move down the hallway, toward the back of the house. Each step she takes brings clarity and strength. Just move, Ona. Just *move*.

She reaches the back door. Maybe the enslaved chef, Hercules, gives her a slight nod; maybe he knows what she's about to do. Then again, maybe he doesn't notice her at all. Ona does not stop. She keeps moving, her breath fast, her vision startlingly clear. Pull the door open. Go outside. Head to the docks. *Move!*

If she is caught . . . *If she is caught* . . .

No. She can't let herself think about that. Not now.

She starts to walk. Or does she run? Does she look back? Does she grimace or frown or smile? We can't know. Security cameras are still hundreds of years in the future. All Ona knows for sure is that she is taking the biggest risk of her life and needs to move quickly to get to the nearby docks built against the banks of the Delaware River. For five city blocks, her head down, her heart probably beating faster than it ever has before, she walks and walks until she ends up on board a ship called the *Nancy*, headed far away.

Ona has no idea where she is going. She has lived with the Washingtons for her entire life. Yet soon, there she is against the ship's railing, alone, wind skimming her face. She is trusting blindly in the white ship captain and her free black friends who have helped her escape. Fear of being caught, of being whipped, of being a slave for the remainder of her life must make her feel like she is wearing a blanket of fire around her neck.

Looking out at the turbulent waves of the Atlantic Ocean, Ona Maria Judge, this brave, trailblazing young woman, has one thought above all else flaming through her mind.

I am free.

CHAPTER ONE

AMERICA'S DAUGHTER

ONA'S STORY BEGINS IN VIRGINIA AROUND 1773, WHEN the United States is not yet the United States, and slavery is considered acceptable by many of the white people who live in what comprises the first thirteen colonies. Strangely enough, the American colonies and the American slaves were engaged in a similar quest for freedom. In 1773 the colonists in America— those people who lived in what would be the original thirteen states of the US—decided they wanted to be free from the British government making all their laws. The enslaved people of America, who had been brought over from Africa and the Caribbean as part of the slave trade, wanted to be free to live as they chose. These fights for freedom as a country and as a race of people would become as much a part of Ona's life as waking up in the morning and breathing.

But first Ona needs to be born.

Ona's parents were Betty, a woman born into slavery in Virginia, and Andrew Judge, a white indentured servant from England whose labor had been bought by George Washington for forty-five dollars. (An indenture agreement meant that in return for Andrew's transport to America, as well as food, clothing, shelter, and a small cash allowance, Andrew's labor was owned for the next four years of his life by whoever purchased his agreement. Still, Andrew had small freedoms as an indentured servant that the enslaved population did not share.) Betty and Andrew were not married. It was illegal for a black person to marry a white person. In fact, it was illegal for slaves to be married at all.

Betty had originally been owned by Daniel Parke Custis, Martha Washington's first husband, who died after only seven years of marriage. By this point in America, slavery was as entrenched as the roots of the biggest, oldest tree. Like the Custises, Martha's family (the Dandridges) owned slaves, as did Martha's second husband's family, the Washingtons. When Daniel died, his property was split three ways between Martha and

ERICA ARMSTRONG DUNBAR and KATHLEEN VAN CLEVE

their children. This property included both land and the humans owned by the Custises—one of whom was Betty, Ona's mother. (This is the reason why Betty was always classified as a "dower" slave meaning that she would always be the property of Martha Washington and her heirs, no matter whom Martha married after Daniel.)

After Martha married George Washington, she brought at least eighty-four slaves with her to Mount Vernon, about one hundred miles away from the main Custis estate. Betty was chosen to go and was allowed to take her two-year-old son, Austin. This was a big deal, because slave families were often split up after the death of the original owner. It may have also indicated that Betty had already established herself as one of Martha's more valued slaves. Certainly by 1773 she had become an important part of Martha Washington's team of seamstresses.

Betty was the person whom many other seamstresses in the Washington household went to when they needed to learn how to hem a skirt or weave a certain fabric. She was also known as the person who could take a piece of expensive material from London and dye it the exact color Martha wanted without ruining the garment. The creation of clothing was an important job for anyone during colonial times, when fabric, not finished clothes, was what was available at a store, and every household needed someone who could use a needle and thread to stitch together garments for everyone—black and white—to wear. Betty's expertise at sewing and spinning kept her out of the fields of George Washington's five working farms. Instead she earned a place working in the spinning house. The spinning house was a building near the mansion where George and Martha lived, where the enslaved seamstresses did their work. Martha herself liked to sew, so sometimes Betty was a part of a larger sewing circle in the mansion, alongside her owner.

Andrew Judge, Ona's father, was also an expert at sewing. Usually George Washington did not prefer white indentured servants. He complained that they were unreliable and lazy, yet George seemed to like and trust Andrew. He was one of George Washington's preferred tailors, eventually creating the blue uniform George wore when he was named commander in chief of the American forces in 1775.

In 1773, however, George would have been surprised to learn that soon he would be leading the American military forces against the British. Although he was a well-known colonel and respected military man, George would have said his main occupation was farming. He was well aware of the political events that

ERICA ARMSTRONG DUNBAR and KATHLEEN VAN CLEVE

were stirring up the anger of the American colonists; he too felt strongly that Americans should not be ruled across an ocean by King George III of England. He knew that many colonists wanted to form a new country with their own form of democratic government. Yet like many of his friends and acquaintances, George had protected British control of American land. Like his father and grandfather, George was also a member of the colonial government in Virginia. Turning publicly against his ancestors and the reigning monarch would be a massive and dangerous step.

Neither George nor the country was quite ready to take such a step. But change was in the air, and it was Mother Nature herself who, by throwing a snowball, got the attention of not only George, but Betty, too.

In June 1773 the unimaginable happened. It snowed in Virginia. Farmers like George Washington needed to rely on familiar weather patterns, but it was anything but familiar for snow to fall this far south in June. Mount Vernon's crops were at risk, and the people on the plantation were confused. Many of the enslaved saw the late snow as an omen bringing something bad upon the people of Mount Vernon. Other enslaved people believed the snow meant that something good was about to happen. Both turned out to be right.

Eight days after the snow fell, Patsy, the daughter

of Martha Washington and her first husband, became terribly ill. Only seventeen, Patsy had been plagued by seizures that had begun during her teenage years. There was no effective treatment for Patsy's condition. Instead the doctors who cared for Patsy would treat her with bloodletting—drawing out her blood as a way to stop the seizures. It never worked.

It was shortly after four o'clock on June 19 when Patsy excused herself after dinner to get a letter from her bedroom. When she didn't come back, her soon-to-be sister-in-law, Eleanor Calvert, went to check on her. Patsy lay on the floor of her room, in the middle of a violent seizure. Though Eleanor called for help immediately, there was very little anyone could do. Within two minutes Patsy was dead.

George Washington, Patsy's stepfather, was devastated. Martha Washington was almost destroyed. When she had been married to her first husband, Martha had borne four children: Daniel, Frances, Jacky, and Patsy. The oldest two children had died when they were toddlers. To lose another child was pushing Martha off an emotional cliff.

In a letter written to his nephew, George Washington stated, "I scarce need add [that Patsy's death] has almost reduced my poor Wife to the lowest ebb of Misery."

ERICA ARMSTRONG DUNBAR and KATHLEEN VAN CLEVE

Everyone at Mount Vernon was aware of Martha's pain, especially the enslaved women whom she had chosen to work near her in the mansion. Betty, Ona's mother, was one of these women.

Only seven years younger than Martha, Betty had already watched Martha as she'd endured the deaths of her first husband and first two children. She understood how painful it was for Martha to lose another child, especially because by this time Betty had two other children besides Austin, and she knew how desperate she would have been if any of them had died.

She may have stood near Martha's bedside, comforting her in her terrible grief while at the same time helping the household prepare for Patsy's funeral. It would not have been relevant to Martha that Betty was pregnant at this time; the fact that she and Andrew Judge were going to have a baby was not and could not be Betty's priority.

We do not know what kind of relationship Andrew and Betty had. They may have fallen in love. They may have had the kind of relationship that is the opposite of love, the kind of nonconsensual encounter where a man uses his strength and privilege to overpower the woman. The truth is that Andrew Judge could have raped Betty, and she would have been unable to do anything about it. His status as a white man would have protected him, just as it did the white male owners who commonly raped the women they owned.

Still, it is also possible that Betty entered into this relationship with aims of her own besides romantic love. Perhaps she believed that having a relationship with Andrew could lead to her own freedom and that of her children, because she knew that in a few years Andrew would become a free man. At that time he could potentially offer to buy all of them from the Washingtons. We will never know Betty's feelings. All we do know is that Andrew Judge did eventually claim his freedom, but he did not take Betty and his child with him. If he loved Betty, it was not enough to keep him from leaving.

Still, in 1773, Andrew was living at Mount Vernon. And sometime during or close to that year, after the strange snowfall and after Patsy's funeral, Betty gave birth to their daughter. They named her Ona Maria Judge. While there are few records about the births and deaths of slaves, this girl child, of mixed race, would, as a young woman, walk that tightrope of freedom for African Americans long before her bold descendants-in-spirit, Harriet Tubman and Frederick Douglass, made their own escapes from slavery.

Like her mother, Betty, Ona learned how to persevere in the face of extreme hardship. Like her father,

ERICA ARMSTRONG DUNBAR and KATHLEEN VAN CLEVE

Ona would eventually free herself no matter who she left behind. Finally, like America itself, Ona would risk everything so that she, too, could achieve those rights written in the Declaration of Independence: life, liberty, and the pursuit of happiness.

CHAPTER TWO

MOUNT VERNON

THE PLACE WHERE ONA GREW UP—MOUNT VERNON—WAS actually an estate owned by George Washington that covered almost eight thousand acres of property in eastern Virginia. George Washington's family had lived in America for four generations; his ancestor John had arrived in America in 1657. The British government believed that since their explorers had landed on the coast of this colony, the British were now the owners of the land, to do whatever they wanted with it. This was news to the Native Americans, who had lived in America for thousands of years, and who had very different ideas about what it meant to "own" land. Still, once the Europeans arrived, the drive to claim more and more land only grew more intense, and soon European countries such as France and England began to fight over which country would control which area in the Americas.

George Washington, like his father and his grandfather, fought for the British government in its quest to claim more land. This is important because when George was a British soldier during the seven-year French and Indian War in the 1750s, he became known to people in England as a worthy military man. He was unafraid to take the lead in battles, and while he experienced hard times—like losing a battle against the French and continuing to fight despite "four bullets through my coat and two horses shot under me"—he also established a reputation for strong, unemotional leadership.

One of the reasons why historians believe George was a good leader in military battles was because of his difficult times growing up. His father died when he was eleven, and he did not get along well with his mother, Mary, who had given birth to five other children. By the time he was sixteen, he was basically living like a grown-up. He never went to college, and he left America only once, in 1751, when he went to Barbados with his older brother Lawrence because it was thought that Lawrence's being in a hotter climate would cure his tuberculosis. It didn't help him, and in fact, while

George was in Barbados, he contracted smallpox. When they returned to Virginia, Lawrence died.

Besides his military battles, George spent most of his time during his thirties and forties building up Mount Vernon. He formed five farms within the one property, growing tobacco, wheat, and flax. The farms were spread across the property—meaning that if you needed to get from one farm to another, you would sometimes have to walk as many as five miles (or go on horseback).

Historians agree that George Washington loved being at Mount Vernon more than any other place on earth. It had become a massive, self-sustaining property. This took much organization and extensive planning. Besides the crops, he had fisheries on the Potomac River, and he had a whiskey distillery near the water. He designed the flower and vegetable gardens throughout the estate; he created a sixteen-sided treading barn to more effectively sweep the wheat berries off the wheat stalks. The wheat berries were then ground up for flour in the gristmill, also on the property. There were farm animals to be raised and used for food, animals like chickens and pigs and cows. There were mules and oxen that were used in the field to pull the heavy plows. George even built a "dung repository," a place where the slaves piled the dung from all the animals so he could experiment with it as fertilizer.

ERICA ARMSTRONG DUNBAR and KATHLEEN VAN CLEVE

George kept detailed records of all his plantation business and was determined to make Mount Vernon a success, completely apart from either his military or his political undertakings. Like all plantation owners in the South, George knew if he exploited the labor of slaves, he would make more money.

George's entire life had been dunked in the miserable water of slavery; he had inherited ten slaves when he was just eleven, when his father died. This number got larger as George grew older and the amount of land he owned spread farther and farther. When he married Martha, who was a widow, he increased his landholdings—and his ownership of the enslaved. By 1773 there were close to two hundred slaves living at Mount Vernon. (Slave owners, including the Washingtons, referred to their human property as "servants," not slaves. Perhaps even way back then, among people who supported slavery wholeheartedly, this choice of words implied that somewhere, deep in their conscience, they knew it was wrong.)

If George wanted to create a gravel pathway in his gardens, he used the enslaved to move the earth and crush the gravel. If he wanted fabric made from linen, he used the enslaved to cut the flax, pull it through steel-nail combs, and eventually spin it to create the thread. If he wanted barrels to be made, or laundry to be washed, or vegetables to be picked, or tools to be forged, he used the enslaved. Mount Vernon became a showplace, for sure, a mansion with a fancy red roof and black iron weather vane that visitors could see from miles away. George was immensely proud of his home and his lands. But if he hadn't owned humans and forced them to do what he wanted, he would not have been as wealthy. George owed his riches to the marginalized enslaved.

Slave owners had the responsibility of building shelters for their slaves. At Mount Vernon these homes were spread throughout George's lands. For slaves like Betty who worked in the mansion, there was a two-story building near the blacksmith's forge called the Quarters or the House for Families. There, up to sixty-seven slaves lived in one building, sleeping in wooden bunk beds on mattresses made of straw and covered with burlap. Children often slept on the floor. Slaves who worked in the fields of the different farms lived in shoddy one- or two-room log cabins. The major difference between the Quarters and the log cabins was that the Quarters was comparatively well made and had a fireplace to generate warmth. The drawback to the Quarters was that for the dozens of slaves who lived there, it was impossible to have any privacy. In the log cabins

ERICA ARMSTRONG DUNBAR and KATHLEEN VAN CLEVE

you suffered through having thin walls that let rain and snow inside, but at least you didn't have to share your bedroom with thirty or forty other people.

George Washington and all other slave owners also had to feed and clothe their slaves. The enslaved who worked in the fields wore clothes made of shabby material. Slaves who worked in the mansion would have more clothing of a slightly better quality (perhaps a patterned dress if you were female, or a colorful jacket if you were male), but only because George was so obsessive about appearance. Excavations at Mount Vernon near the slave quarters have shown a root cellar, where slaves stored their vegetables after the harvest. They used utensils and dinnerware that were hand-me-downs from the Washingtons. Adult slaves received one pair of shoes. Children often went barefoot.

When Ona was born, the value of Martha's estate, the property that she owned and would pass on to her grandchildren, would have increased. Every slave was considered property; therefore, every enslaved baby was more property—and worth more money. George thought of himself as a benevolent slave owner. He often said that he did not like separating slave families and he believed that slaves who had grown older had to be taken care of by him. Still, he did separate slave families when he felt it was necessary, even selling slaves away from Mount Vernon altogether and sometimes sending them to the brutal sugar and coffee plantations of the Caribbean.

Despite sugar's "sweet" reputation, sugar plantations were quite literally the opposite—perhaps the most brutal of all the slave-labor-filled enterprises. Slaves who were sent to sugar plantations in the Caribbean died an average of seven years after their arrival. Like other plantation owners, George approved of whippings if he believed this dehumanizing punishment would compel a slave to get in line.

This was the world Ona entered when she was born in 1773. Her owner was legally Martha Washington, but George, like most males at the time, was in charge of his wife's property. Ona lived in the Quarters, probably wearing one shift or dress day after day, and slept on the floor. One of the older slave women would have watched her with the other children during the day when Betty worked. All the slaves, male or female, whether they worked inside the mansion or out in one of the fields, worked from sunup to sundown. If Ona got sick, she would not be able to curl up next to her mother for comfort; if she wanted to ask her mother a question or show her something new she had learned, she would have to wait until it got dark. Probably even

ERICA ARMSTRONG DUNBAR and KATHLEEN VAN CLEVE

then, Ona would fall asleep before Betty came home.

As Ona grew into a bushy-haired child, with light skin and freckles, she—like all the other children—would have had no choice but to learn to fend for herself. Often the children would be asked to do chores like gathering sticks for fires or fetching water for the mansion house. She may have had to work in the garden, helping to pull ripe vegetables from the ground, or she may have watched the spinners in the spinning house as they carefully threaded the flax strands over the big spinning wheels. For sure, Ona would have learned to steer clear of the overseers who were supervising the work of the slaves. She would have already received her first "lessons" about how to behave in front of her owners and would have been advised by her mother about how she should stand and sit and speak and look down.

Ona would not have to go to school. There were no schools in Virginia for young enslaved children. In fact, it was illegal to teach enslaved people how to read or write in the South. Martha believed that black people were morally and intellectually inferior to white people, and while she sometimes formed close relationships with individual slaves, she never doubted the value of slavery as an institution that could preserve her way of life.

But by the early 1770s, America was changing

fast. Ona was going to spend her childhood with a front-row seat to not only the literal battlegrounds of the Revolutionary War, but also to the battle of ideas sparked by the formation of a brand-new country. Ona was barely a one-year-old child when the First Continental Congress began in September 1774. When George left Mount Vernon to attend this meeting in Philadelphia, he didn't know he was headed to an event that would set the stage for the two sides in the Revolutionary War. Martha didn't know that by the end of the upcoming war, her entire sense of the world as a place of slave owners and slaves would be challenged. And Ona didn't know that she was going to have her own battle of ideas in her head, and that the outcome would surprise everyone, especially her.

CHAPTER THREE

THE NEW COUNTRY

ON JUNE 15, 1775, GEORGE WASHINGTON WAS ELECTED commander of the Continental Army. Tensions between the Americans and the British had grown worse, and when George was approached by John Adams and asked to lead the troops, he had already made up his mind. He agreed to the military appointment and gave his loyalty to the Americans. By doing so, he turned away, as publicly as possible, from his British heritage. In a matter of days, George was on his way to Boston to battle Britain for the first time. He did not return to Mount Vernon for more than six years.

Ona was about two years old when George left Mount Vernon. When the British surrendered to the

Americans in 1781 after the battle at Yorktown, Ona was eight and still a child. But she would have been affected—as was the entire community of people living at Mount Vernon—by George's absence and by the war itself. George had appointed a relative of his, Lund Washington, to run the estate in his absence. Martha, never a shy woman, shadowed Lund and monitored his decisions, knowing that George would always take her side if there was a dispute.

This was a time when letter writing was the only possible form of communication between people who lived great distances from one another. George's letters to Lund and other people are what allow us to know what he was thinking about when he was leading the American army and trying to maintain control of his plantation. While George wrote letters to Martha regularly, these letters are no longer able to be studied. Before her death, Martha burned most of her correspondence with her husband. She gave no explanation for why she did this.

The Revolutionary War was fought up and down the eastern coast of the United States. In fact, George Washington was not in Philadelphia when Congress approved the Declaration of Independence on July 4, 1776. He was fighting in New York. Instead he read the declaration to his troops from the battlefield on

ERICA ARMSTRONG DUNBAR and KATHLEEN VAN CLEVE

July 9. The battles continued over the years in New York, New Jersey, and Pennsylvania, and down to Virginia. Martha sometimes traveled to the battlegrounds to see George and was able to observe for herself the extreme suffering of the soldiers and her husband. Often there was not enough food, or clothing, or shelter for the army. George had begged the Congress to supply more money and weapons, but these were slow in arriving, if they came at all.

The British had a huge advantage in terms of supplies, manpower, and wealth. Yet they still had to do all their fighting across an ocean from their homeland, in a place they did not know. This was one of the reasons why they initiated a sly strategy when they began to fight against the Americans. They communicated through newspapers and town centers that any slaves in America who escaped their owners to fight with the British would be freed by the British after the war.

Enslaved people always wanted to be free. Lund Washington had even written this to George in a letter, stating that all the slaves at Mount Vernon would leave "if they believe'd they could make their escape. . . . Liberty is sweet." The slaves of Mount Vernon had their chance in April 1781. A British ship called the HMS *Savage* parked on the Potomac River in sight of Mount Vernon. All the people living on the plantation would have been aware of the ship, especially when British soldiers intentionally set fire to several homes on the opposite side of the river, in clear view of Mount Vernon. Ona, just eight, may have been outside with some of the other enslaved children, wide-eyed when she saw the flames erupting from the nearby homes. She may have even overheard Lund talking about the letter he had received from Captain Richard Graves, threatening to burn down Mount Vernon if Lund didn't bring "provisions" to his ship. ("Provisions" is a fancy way of saying "food.")

That afternoon, when Lund walked down to the river with a load of chickens, Ona would have been near the other slaves—adults and children—watching every move. With Lund far away the slaves would have been whispering about the opportunity that was right there in front of them: escape, right now, at this very second. Three women—Lucy, who was twenty; Esther, who was eighteen; and Deborah, who was sixteen—may have locked eyes with one another while Ona stared at them, sure that something exhilarating, and terrifying, was about to happen.

After Lund returned from the HMS *Savage* and went back to his home, the three young women, along with fourteen men, made a desperate dash for freedom.

ERICA ARMSTRONG DUNBAR and KATHLEEN VAN CLEVE

They boarded the British ship that remained parked outside the general's home, hoping that emancipation had finally come their way. Ona may have been there, watching as one of the older enslaved women hissed that the runaways were being foolish, while another slave may have looked at the runaways with envy, perhaps telling Ona to pray for them because they were taking the biggest risk of their lives, with the highest possible reward.

Lund was furious when he learned that the slaves had run away. He was already at his limit, trying to run this massive plantation; he was not a man of entrepreneurial vision like his cousin George. He often didn't feel up to the job of running Mount Vernon, and he was right. Without the labor of these seventeen slaves, his life was going to get even worse. He went back to the *Savage* with a huge amount of food and supplies, thinking he could swap these for the return of the slaves. But Captain Graves refused. Lund returned to Mount Vernon distraught.

It didn't help that the Marquis de Lafayette, a close friend of George's who was in Virginia, wrote a letter to George, telling him about the escaped slaves and how Lund had brought food and supplies to the British. George was furious. In his next letter to Lund, he berated his cousin for talking to the British at all, telling him that he would have preferred for the British to light Mount Vernon on fire rather than give the British any provisions. He didn't mention the escaped slaves.

Even at eight years old, Ona would have known enough to avoid Lund. But she would never forget the vision of the burning houses on the other side of the river, or the escaping slaves, or the expressions of the slaves who remained. What Ona could not have known—and neither did Lund—was that the British troops in Virginia were in big trouble. Besides the fact that the French, with the Marquis de Lafayette, had come to the aid of the Americans, smallpox and malaria were racing through the campsites of the British soldiers both on land and at sea. British captains were forced to stop new soldiers (enslaved and otherwise) from joining them because they didn't want more soldiers to get sick. At the same time, food supplies were dwindling.

By October 1781 George Washington had arrived in Virginia and was entering into a battle at Yorktown, with a lot of help from the French. The French, led by Lafayette, and the Americans, led by Washington, had trapped the British by corralling them. The number of healthy British soldiers was far less than the approximately sixteen thousand American and French forces. It was simply too much for the British to continue the

ERICA ARMSTRONG DUNBAR and KATHLEEN VAN CLEVE

fight. On October 17, 1781, the leader of the British troops in Yorktown, Lord Cornwallis, sent a young man over to the Americans with a white flag. He walked to the middle of the grounds and began to wave the flag in a gesture that meant the British were surrendering. Two days later, when Cornwallis signed the articles of surrender, the American colonists won the war and the right to become an independent nation.

This was fantastic news for the colonists, who had put their entire futures on the line by fighting for their freedom from the British. This was awful news for the enslaved who had put their entire futures on the line by fighting for their freedom from the colonists. After the British surrendered, they completely abandoned the escaped American slaves. It was a wretched time for these people who had risked everything for their freedom. Seven of the seventeen slaves from Mount Vernon, including Esther and Lucy, were returned there. They were skinny, desperate, and devastated.

Ona would have been there when the seven escaped slaves were returned. She would have seen Esther and Lucy and the others in the flesh, defeated. She would also learn, later, how George was intent on finding the other slaves who had escaped, paying people such as the army veteran and slave catcher named Daniel Parker to hunt them down in Philadelphia, where George believed they were hiding. Ona would remember how shattered the escaped slaves were upon their capture and return to Mount Vernon.

Meanwhile, even though the British had surrendered, it still took time for the war to wind down. The official document that declared the war over—the Treaty of Paris—was signed on September 3, 1783. George Washington heard this news with measured joy; despite the hardships and deaths of his fellow soldiers, he had accomplished the impossible and now could go home. In December he officially resigned from the military. Soon he was on his way back to Mount Vernon.

The war had definitely changed him. For eight and a half years, George had led about one hundred thousand men who everyone—including, sometimes, George—thought would lose to the British. There were never enough shoes, blankets, or shirts for the men who fought; even gunpowder had been hard to find. Nearly twenty-five thousand soldiers had died. The physical and psychological scars that had been inflicted on the surviving soldiers would burden them—and their families—for the rest of their lives.

George Washington was permanently affected too. Memories of his happy life at Mount Vernon had sustained him throughout the war. He understood that he had surprised the entire world by leading the Americans

ERICA ARMSTRONG DUNBAR and KATHLEEN VAN CLEVE

to victory against the British. But he was not dancing around in the streets in triumph. There had been another personal heartbreak soon after the Battle of Yorktown. After many years of not taking work seriously, Jacky, Martha's only surviving child, had gone to Yorktown to act as an aide to his stepfather. While there, Jacky had caught an infectious disease called "camp fever" that had been spreading through the campgrounds of both the American and British troops. Hundreds of soldiers had died; Jacky was one of them. He'd been only twenty-seven years old. Jacky's wife, Eleanor Calvert (the woman who long ago had found his sister Patsy dying upstairs in Mount Vernon) was back at their home, with their four very young children. George knew that Martha would be suffering, and he was even more intent on getting back to Mount Vernon to be by her side.

Still, even when he rode up to his beloved home and sat on his porch overlooking the beautiful Potomac River, George knew that the new country, like a newborn baby, would need more help to survive. During and after the war, the Congress had come up with a document called the Articles of Confederation, which was supposed to outline the rules that all the states had to follow now that they were united as one country. The states had agreed to this when they'd all been fighting against one enemy: the British. Now that the British had gone home, the states realized that they had merely postponed many problems boiling up between the states themselves.

One of the major issues was what to do about a ruler. The United States had just fought a war and lost thousands of lives because they did not want one supreme ruler, like a king or queen. All states should have the right to decide for themselves what was acceptable, people argued. The notion of working as one country with a central "federal" government that enacted laws for the entire country was not seen as important.

This issue fed into the smoldering debate between the states about slavery. The states in the South had more money because they didn't pay the enslaved who actually produced the products that earned them money. The North, without the same kind of economy, owed a lot of money, particularly to France, who had agreed to align itself with the Americans in their war against the British. France needed to be paid. The war had been fought on behalf of all the states, not just the northern ones. But the Articles of Confederation did not spell out rules for the new country to act as one country, especially in terms of money. The founders were still too fearful that one leader—like a king—would emerge to tell everyone what to do. This meant that the new country's laws did not serve *one* country at all, but thirteen individual states. In situations where it was clear that the amount of money

ERICA ARMSTRONG DUNBAR and KATHLEEN VAN CLEVE

owed was more than any one state could pay, there were no consequences for another state that said it didn't want to contribute to their debt, even though the debt was incurred on behalf of all the states. (There are even some lines in the smash hit musical *Hamilton* about this: "Your debts are paid cuz you don't pay for labor. 'We plant seeds in the South. We create.' Yeah, keep ranting. We know who's really doing the planting.")

Changes were necessary. The problems ignored during the Revolutionary War would have to be addressed. George Washington knew this but chose, for a while anyway, to ignore it. Probably when he returned to his expansive estate, with its well-run farms and beautiful gardens, he believed that Mount Vernon, with its beauty and grace, was his refuge from all that was unpleasant. When he looked at the humans he owned as property, particularly the young barefoot girl named Ona (but whom he called Oney) running around the Quarters, it likely never crossed his mind that she would one day grow up and challenge him and the institution of slavery as blatantly as if she had stood in front of him right then, in her little shift dress, and told him that like the new country, she wanted to be free.

For now, in 1781, George probably rode up and gave his horse to one of his slaves to lead to the stables. If he paid attention to any of the enslaved children, there is no record of it.

CHAPTER FOUR

THE LIST

IT WAS ABOUT TWO YEARS AFTER THE BATTLE OF YORKTOWN when Martha motioned for Ona to follow her to the mansion. It was time for her to officially go to work. She was ten years old.

Martha had been watching Ona ever since she was born. She probably saw how quickly Ona could follow instructions, how well she behaved in front of others. Martha already knew how important Ona's mother, Betty, was to her well-being, but Betty also had four children. Ona would have no distractions. She would be trained, from the outset, to focus only and always on one person: Martha Washington herself.

It is hard to imagine what it would be like for a

young girl who is ushered into a mansion and told she is now going to personally attend to the owner. Maybe Ona was scared or maybe she was calm, since her own mother would have warned her about this day. Ona had spent much of the previous ten years hanging around the spinning house, where Betty had taught her how to sew hems and seams, thread needles, and make tiny, perfect stitches in a straight line. She probably already knew how to wind the strands of homemade thread on the spinning wheels, trying to avoid the pointy end of the staff, or else end up with the blood from her pricked finger staining one of the garments.

Ona would have noticed that the seamstresses' work seemed to be endless. Their job was to provide suitable clothing for everyone on the plantation, including all two hundred slaves. This was in addition to the specific work a favored slave like Betty did for Martha directly. Washing Martha's clothing, preparing the dresses that Martha had selected, sewing new clothes that Martha wanted, scrubbing out mud stains on the skirts, and repairing gloves and bonnets were all part of Betty's work. Now some of this work would become Ona's.

Meanwhile, without battles and shoeless soldiers and freezing weather, George spent his time the way he loved best. He rode out to his fields and considered different, better ways of earning more money from Mount Vernon. He built his fisheries and inspected his distillery and looked at the giant leaves of the tobacco plants for evidence of hornworms. But George could not remove himself from the politics of the new nation even if he tried. George, like many others, believed that the Articles needed to be revised for the sake of unity as well as to address the more basic concern of having one standard monetary value for everyday items like flour or fabric. Each state, for example, had its own currency, which made it really hard to figure out the cost of anything that would be sold over a state border. Did the fabric cost a Virginia dollar per yard or a Pennsylvania dollar? No one knew.

Men such as Alexander Hamilton, James Madison, and Edmund Randolph decided the time had come to try something new. They called for a Constitutional Convention and requested that every state in the new country send representatives. In 1787 George Washington was invited to go to Philadelphia as part of Virginia's delegation. He went, along with his most favored slave, William Lee, who served George as a kind of butler called a "valet." That summer in Philadelphia all thirteen states agreed—after a tremendous amount of infighting—on a new governing document called the Constitution of the United States, which detailed the guidelines for developing a stronger central (also called "federal") government.

When it was finally signed in September, no one, least of all George, knew whether the document would be strong yet flexible enough to cover the issues of an entire nation, now and in the future.

When he left Philadelphia, George felt trapped for a different reason. During the convention, and after endless discussions and fights, the representatives had finally agreed that there should, in fact, be a leader of the new country. "The executive Power shall be vested in a President of the United States of America," states Article II, Section 1 of the United States Constitution.

The men who attended the convention determined that the way to organize the federal government was to break it up into three branches. The first branch, the legislative part, was to be made up of senators and congressmen from every state. This branch would create the laws. Most women and African Americans were not allowed to vote, and no women were elected to a congressional office.

The second branch, the judicial, was to be made up of judges, who would serve on the court until they died. This branch would decide whether people were abiding by or had broken laws.

The final branch would be the executive branch.

There would be one leader, called the president. This president would be elected in the same way as the congressmen and senators—by the people of the new country.

The idea behind the three branches was that none of the three would be able to wrest so much power that there would be a repeat of what had happened in England with a king—or elsewhere, with rulers called dictators. Still, there was no question that the person who would be president of the new country would have a tremendous amount of power over the lives of Americans. It was critical to choose a person with wisdom, experience, intelligence, vision, and compassion. George probably knew as soon as this clause was written that he was the most likely person to be elected president. While today it is clear that George's ownership of slaves was immoral, at the time he was one of the most respected men in the country—the only man with, it seemed, this particular mix of character traits. George was not falsely humble; he expected to be chosen.

He was right.

On April 14, 1789, Charles Thomson, secretary of the Continental Congress, arrived on horseback at Mount Vernon. He informed George that he had been unanimously elected to serve as president, having

ERICA ARMSTRONG DUNBAR and KATHLEEN VAN CLEVE

captured all sixty-nine electoral votes. Thomson read him a letter written by Senator John Langdon of New Hampshire that basically said he hoped George would agree to the position, especially because it was a sign of how much people in the new country admired him.

Duty was calling; Mount Vernon would have to wait. Despite mounting concerns about the financial health of his plantation—poor harvests and overdue taxes had left even him, the newly elected president, with little cash, George left Mount Vernon for New York just two days later, on April 16, 1789. Fear, regret, and concern spilled onto the pages of the president's diary.

> *About ten o'clock, I bade adieu to Mount Vernon, to private life, and to domestic felicity; and with a mind oppressed with more anxious and painful sensations than I have words to express.*

For sure, George was worried about whether the new nation would succeed. This would make anyone anxious. But he was troubled for another reason as well. He was going to New York alone.

Martha was mad. She wrote about her feelings to her niece Fanny Bassett.

I am truly sorry to tell you that the
General is gone to New York. . . . When,
or whether, he will ever come home
again, God only knows. I think it
was much too late for him to enter into
public life again, but it was not to be
avoided. Our family will be deranged,
as I must soon follow him.

Her life was being turned upside down, again, like
when George had agreed to lead America's military.
Again George was choosing public duty over personal contentment, and again Martha's desires were
not part of his decision making. Martha did not like
the North. She was comfortable in Virginia among
people she had known for her entire life. Yet she was
also aware that no matter how upset she was, she did
not want to live away from George. She loved him
and wanted to be with him; she just needed some
time to get used to the idea of moving.

Martha also had to grapple with a bigger problem.
She knew that the issue of slavery became more intense
during the years after the Revolutionary War. Indeed,
one of the biggest fights during the Constitutional
Convention was over the representation of slaves in
the Constitution. The final document stated that slaves

would be counted as "three fifths of all other Persons." It is impossible to read this today without feeling sick because it is difficult to understand how the government agreed to count humans as less than human.

Even then, there were many Americans, mostly in the North, who found this shameful. Pennsylvania, Massachusetts, and Connecticut had begun to enact state laws that restricted slavery. There were rumblings about barring slavery altogether in the new nation, on moral grounds. Every state in the North was having these conversations, including New York, Martha's future home. No matter how much Martha supported the institution of slavery, she knew she was headed straight into the lion's den when she moved with her husband northward.

At no moment did Martha ever consider living a life without her slaves in the North. This made it even more important that she and George choose with great care the slaves who would travel with them from Mount Vernon. They wanted the dutiful slaves who listened to them without argument, the ones who were seen as loyal and therefore less likely to escape.

Martha would have known George's preference for slaves of mixed race. George believed that interracial slaves were more attractive and more intelligent. William Lee, the slave that George had taken with him to Philadelphia in 1787 and who was currently with him in New York, was of mixed race. Indeed, William Lee was the only slave who left Mount Vernon on April 16, 1789, to go to New York with the new president. He was as close to George Washington as any slave could be to an owner.

It took Martha several weeks, but eventually she was able to put aside her resentment about moving and start to assemble the group of enslaved people to take with her to New York. The criteria were clear: obedient, discreet, loyal slaves, preferably of mixed race.

Ona Judge was the first name on her list.

CHAPTER FIVE

THE FIRST TRIP NORTH

BY THE TIME MARTHA MADE HER LIST, ONA HAD WORKED for her in the mansion for nearly six years. She had shown herself to be exceedingly competent, anticipating Martha's needs even before Martha knew what they were. Ona was quietly efficient at sewing, and she was smart. She would have known that when Martha was compiling her list of people to take with her to New York, the overseers and the Washingtons were watching her every move to be sure she was not insolent or disrespectful or lazy. Ona would have known that Martha would accompany George for his new job. What Ona did not know, and could not know, was how it would affect her.

It is impossible to know how familiar Ona and the other slaves at Mount Vernon were with the simmering conflict over the institution of slavery in the new country. The concept of emancipation—that is, freedom—was alive in the minds of all of the enslaved. They would remember the slaves who had escaped to the HMS *Savage*, and they would remember the haggard looks of the captured runaways when they'd been forcibly returned. Ona would know the stories of runaways throughout the years who had never been heard from again—as well as the stories of those who'd been captured and disciplined by a severe whipping or some other form of horrific punishment. Definitely she would be aware that trying to escape carried with it a risk of immense suffering, and often death.

At the same time, it is certain that the idea that there was freedom somewhere in the North had reached the ears of the slaves. It is not hard to understand how the fantasy of living freely was the happiest of daydreams for people like Ona.

Unfortunately, slaves did not have much time to daydream. It didn't ultimately matter what Ona knew about the North, or whether she wanted to stay at Mount Vernon. As an enslaved person, she had no rights, no possibility of stalling until she had gotten her head around leaving her home, and few outlets

ERICA ARMSTRONG DUNBAR and KATHLEEN VAN CLEVE

to express sorrow about leaving her mother. The fear of the unknown, the separation from her family, and the forced relocation to a state far away in the North must have been overwhelming. But once Martha decreed that Ona was going with her to New York, Ona had no choice but to keep quiet and prepare for their departure. It is hard for most teenagers to hold in their emotions, but for teenage slaves it did not matter. Ona kept her mouth shut even as her thoughts must have raged.

The only other enslaved woman chosen to go with the Washingtons was a fifty-year-old seamstress named Moll. Perhaps Ona looked at her as a friend, but given their thirty-four-year age difference, this was unlikely. Ona would not have someone she could confide in during this journey. She undoubtedly had "friends" among other teenage slaves, but these friendships would be unfamiliar to kids today. Enslaved children and teenagers could not spend time together; they could not laugh and gossip together, except in secret or sometimes while they were working. They could not choose when they would be able to tell each other stories or share a meal or do any of the other things that make people nurture close friendships. But what's amazing is that they still managed to form meaningful relationships.

Ona would have known white children. Both Martha and George had large families who liked to spend time at Mount Vernon. Ona would have grown up with them—people like Martha's oldest grandchild, Eliza Custis, who was just three years younger than Ona, as well as, perhaps, Martha's niece and nephew, the siblings Fanny and Burwell Bassett, to whom Martha was especially close. They would certainly have known Ona, but even if they liked her or thought she was smart, they could not have been her friends as we understand the term. Owners and the enslaved did not mix socially. More relevant, Ona would have had little time for friendships. If anything, she would have had to watch over her peers like Eliza, Martha's granddaughter, who was known to be a spoiled brat.

In New York, Ona and Moll would serve as housemaids and personal attendants to Martha. Ona would be her primary attendant, while Moll would be in charge of the two grandchildren that Martha and George were raising. (Martha's son Jacky had four children before he died, and the two youngest, ten-year-old Eleanor Parke Custis—called "Nelly"—and eight-year-old George Washington Parke Custis—called "Washy"—had moved in with the Washingtons.) Ona already knew that during her "free" time, she would be helping Moll with the grandchildren. Likely, she never thought her life in New York would be anything but exhausting. It was a privilege of freedom to be able to think about things like talking to a friend, enjoying leisure time, or appreciating the curiosities of a new city.

The other slaves chosen to go to New York were all male. Besides William Lee (who was already in New York with the president), two men, named Giles and Paris, were going to serve as postilions to the Washingtons. That is, they would drive the horse-drawn carriages from atop a horse. The other slaves chosen to move to New York were Christopher Sheels and Ona's half brother Austin. They would be waiters for the Washingtons, trained by William himself. The fact that Christopher was William's family member would have made him an easy choice. And like Ona, her brother Austin was a favored slave of both Martha and George. Unfortunately for Austin, he would be leaving his chosen wife, Charlotte, and his children at Mount Vernon. While the president was a fan of Austin's, he did not like Charlotte. She was known for her sarcastic tongue and general stubbornness. George and Martha were probably grateful that she would not be around to annoy them in their new home. They did not care that Austin would be separated from his family; the foundation of slavery was that a slave's responsibility was to his or her owner, not their family.

On May 14, 1789, Robert Lewis, George and Martha's twenty-year-old nephew, arrived at Mount Vernon to escort his aunt and her slaves to New York. It had not even occurred to him that Martha wouldn't be ready. But she wasn't. Instead of an organized group of people and belongings, he found a frenzied and hectic scene. "Everything appeared to be in confusion," he wrote in his diary. When the departure finally took place on May 16, Robert described the emotional moment for the slaves and Martha:

> After an early dinner and making all necessary arrangements in which we were greatly retarded, it brought us to 3 o'clock in the afternoon when we left Mt. V. The servants of the house, and a number of the field negroes made their appearance—to take leave of their mistress—numbers of these poor wretches seemed greatly agitated, much affected—My Aunt equally so.

ERICA ARMSTRONG DUNBAR and KATHLEEN VAN CLEVE

Betty, Ona's mother, must have been one of those agitated, affected slaves. Like Ona, she could not complain. But like mothers throughout time, it would have been heartbreaking to watch her children prepare to leave their home. Betty had never had complete control over the lives of her children—no enslaved mother did—but to watch Ona and Austin depart with Martha for a new and strange part of the country must have been unbearable, another cruel and very public slap in the face. Would Ona and Austin come back? Would she ever see her children again? Betty had no power; she would have to wait for the answers.

On her journey north Ona was also probably full of questions when she finally pushed back the wall of fear in her heart. Where would she sleep? What would the house be like? How different would the work be? Ona had only lived at Mount Vernon, where there were three times as many black people as white people, even though all of them were enslaved. William Lee, George Washington's valet, had already told them that in the North there were more white people living side by side, and it was all supposed to be very crowded. What about looking at expanses of fields? What about the joy Ona may have felt when she was running errands and paused for just a second to look at a flower or a particularly beautiful tree? What about all the people whom she knew and who knew her?

None of that mattered. The priority was always Martha. This was proven during every minute of their journey. Martha and her grandchildren sat in the top-of-the-line British-made carriage, painted with scenes of the seasons on all the doors. They sat on comfortable green silk cushions. There was a roof on the carriage, and it had wheels that were from Germany—which eased the travel on the unpaved roads between Virginia and Maryland.

Meanwhile, the male slaves, and Robert Lewis himself, all rode on horseback. Ona and Moll were in a small "chariot." However, the word "chariot" makes it sound better than what it really was. They had to stand, there was no roof, and it would bump and jostle at every stone and dip in the ground. The baggage was piled high on a wagon.

The first hurdle for the procession was crossing the Potomac by barge ferry to Georgetown, Maryland. (This meant that the carriages and chariot would be loaded onto a long, rectangular flat-bottomed barge and rowed across the river to the other side.) The horses that had taken them this far would be released, because George Washington had arranged for fresh horses to be waiting for them on the other side.

Martha and her grandchildren went first; the slaves followed on another barge. But the new horses didn't like the harness and recoiled, leaping back and trying to run away. By this point Martha had taken her grandchildren to a nearby tavern to wait. Ona may have gone with her, but she may have stayed and she may have watched as the coachmen proceeded to lash the horses with their whips so that they would behave. Eventually the horses were strapped into their halters and the procession began anew. Before arriving in Baltimore, the group stopped again, this time at a place called Spurrier's Tavern. Martha was led inside, followed by Ona, who wheeled Martha's trunk.

Traveling, even within a carriage with green silk cushions, was dusty. Every speck of Martha's clothes would have been covered in sediment from the roads. Naturally, every speck of Ona's, Moll's, Austin's, and Christopher Sheels's clothes were covered in dust too, but cleaning up their clothes was not a priority. Cleaning Martha's clothes was, as always, what was most important.

Inside the tavern Ona would have opened the trunk and shaken out one of Martha's riding dresses. She would have helped Martha out of her first dress, and she would have had to shake that out too and repack it in the trunk. She would have removed Martha's bonnet and combed out her hair. Within hours they were on their way again.

Baltimore was the first time on this trip when it became incredibly clear that Martha was now a celebrity. It must have been fascinating for Ona to watch the attention poured onto her owner by so many strangers. A whole host of people—men and women—had met her outside Baltimore to escort her into the city. She was staying at the home of James and Margaret McHenry. James had been a Revolutionary War aide to both George and Lafayette. That night there was a fireworks presentation, and later on, at two in the morning, a serenade.

Ona and Moll probably stayed with the McHenrys' slaves in their slave quarters. They may have been able to watch the fireworks too, although only as a side benefit when they were minding the grandchildren.

The group left at five the next morning so that they could avoid any parade that might be intended. This was not because Martha did not like the attention. It was because she could not wait to get to Philadelphia and to the home of her friends Robert and Mary Morris. The passengers were going to spend almost five days in Philadelphia before heading to their final destination, New York City, on Monday, May 25.

Given her low expectations about black people,

Martha would have been surprised to know how much the very word "Philadelphia" excited her fellow travelers. But Philadelphia had long been in the minds of Ona and all the slaves; the stories they had heard from William Lee had engaged their fantasies ever since they'd left Mount Vernon, especially the fact that, unlike most slaves, he had come so very close to being part of his own romantic fairy tale with a woman named Margaret.

Ona had never met Margaret, but her story loomed large in Ona's mind. William had told the other slaves that long ago, when he had traveled with George to Philadelphia for the Continental Congress, he had discovered that many black men and women lived freely and were paid for their work. (This, too, added to the fairy-tale aspect of the story.) One of these free black women was named Margaret Thomas. William had fallen in love quickly, and so, apparently, had Margaret. Even though a marriage between them would have been illegal, George had supposedly given permission for Margaret to move to Mount Vernon to be with William.

Sadly, William Lee had returned alone. (A side note to this story is that before William Lee had gone to Philadelphia for the first time, he had been called "Billy" by everyone, including George Washington himself. In Philadelphia something happened that made him decide to use his full name. He proceeded to tell everyone, including George, to refer to him as William. We cannot know for sure, but it is likely that living among free blacks had influenced this decision—along with his meeting Margaret.)

Margaret never lived at Mount Vernon. No one knows whether she ever even tried to make the trip or whether she decided, ultimately, that her freedom was more important to her than true love and stayed in Philadelphia. It would have been incredibly dangerous for her, a free woman, to move to a state where slavery was the norm. She would also have known that she would be different from the enslaved. For example, she may have known how to read and write, which was not true for most slaves. (Young Christopher Sheels, on horseback in front of Ona, did, and this made him a rarity.) This, among other reasons, may have been why she did not end up at Mount Vernon.

William Lee was never given a letter or even told what had happened to this woman who had affected him so deeply. It was a heartbreak for William that opened the door to a string of sad events—he was injured in 1785, shattering his knee, and again in 1788, when on a cold and snowy day he slipped and shattered his other knee. Still, George Washington agreed to bring William to New York as a member of his team of slaves, even though William's injuries prevented him from arriving in New York until June 22, 1789, more than two months after George.

Ona, too, had a while to go before she reached New York. Her next stop was the place that would prove to be her transformative home: Philadelphia.

CHAPTER SIX

A SHORT STAY IN PHILADELPHIA

ONA WALKED OUT OF PHILADELPHIA FOR THE LAST TIME IN May 1796. She walked into it for the first time in May 1789, seven years earlier. Her entire life had been spent in a place of wide lawns, chirping birds, vast fields, and large houses. Now she woke up in a place where everyone seemed to live within an inch of one another, where the noise of the thousands of humans overwhelmed any bird sounds, where the houses were narrow, the ground was covered in cobblestones, and astonishingly, free black people moved among free white people. It must have felt as if the Washingtons had placed her smack in the middle of a new galaxy, without any guidebook to help her on her way.

Ona was a quick learner, which was a good thing. There was a lot to learn.

For starters, in 1789, Philadelphia was the largest city in the country, by a long shot. In Fairfax County, Virginia—where Mount Vernon was based—the total population was 12,320 people, of which more than 4,500 were enslaved. But Mount Vernon did not make up all of Fairfax County, so the number of people around Ona on the plantation was approximately three hundred, and about two hundred of them were enslaved. It was a fact of her early life in Virginia that there were always more black people than white people. The landscape at Mount Vernon was vast enough that the only location where Ona may have felt crowded was in the Quarters. Otherwise the land was the expansive factor in her life, not people.

It was the opposite in Philadelphia. There the total population was close to forty-four thousand residents. (This number included the suburbs.) Of this number—all of whom lived within the boundaries of the city limits—just 273 were slaves. About 1,800 black men and women were free. The city was a leader in everything at this point in American history—population, businesses, shipping—but what is striking to realize today is that Philadelphia was far out in front of other states in the abolition movement. ("Abolition" means the act of ending an institution or system—such as slavery.)

Slavery as an institution was much more widespread in the South. By the time of the first American census in 1790, the number of slaves living in the southern states dwarfed the number living in the North.

REGION	TOTAL POPULATION	TOTAL SLAVES
The North (Massachusetts, New Hampshire, Rhode Island, Connecticut, New York, New Jersey, Pennsylvania, Delaware)	1,845,169	49,241 (3%)
The South (North Carolina, South Carolina, Virginia, Maryland, Georgia)	1,543,637	525,499 (34%)

Source: Census of the United States, 1790

The states in the South could sell their cash crops—tobacco, rice, and sugar—all around the world for profit. While planting and growing food occurred throughout the new United States, the climate in the southern states enabled the growing season to last almost all year round. The northern states, on the other hand, had a shorter growing season because of their longer and colder winters.

By the time George and Martha Washington were born in 1732 and 1731 respectively, slavery had become as much a part of their worldview as the fact that the

ERICA ARMSTRONG DUNBAR and KATHLEEN VAN CLEVE

sun came up in the morning. The president and his wife had been brought up as children to believe that owning people of color was okay, just as it was acceptable that it was easier for them to achieve prosperity because they had been born into a prosperous family. What a child believes, however, often changes as new experiences and new people are encountered. It is true to say that slavery was acceptable in the 1700s. Some people—Martha Washington, for example—liked it this way and would not change their mind. Other people, like George, started to shift their thinking.

Another person who rethought his position on slavery was one of the most famous people in the United States *not* named George Washington, the guy who lived right around the corner from Martha's hosts in Philadelphia.

His name? Benjamin Franklin.

Benjamin Franklin was twenty-five years older than the Washingtons. Like them, he had owned slaves during his life. He had been born in Boston in 1706, moved to Philadelphia in 1723, and begun to work as a printer, one of his many professions. Benjamin was known for being a practical man who worked hard, saved money, and was fun to be around.

Benjamin once said, "For having lived long, I have experienced many instances of being obliged by better information, or fuller consideration, to change opinions even on important subjects, which I once thought right, but found to be otherwise."

In other words, he wasn't afraid to change his mind.

The chipping away at Franklin's belief in slavery began, it seems, around 1760, when he became a member of Bray Associates—an organization dedicated to founding schools for black children. (Absalom Jones, a famous black leader in Philadelphia, had briefly attended one of these schools.) In 1763 Franklin visited one of the schools and wrote a letter confirming that he saw no intellectual difference between white and black children. By 1775—the year before he left the United States for France—he wrote that black people are "not deficient in natural Understanding, but they have not the Advantage of Education." When he returned to Pennsylvania in 1785, he became a member of the Society for the Relief of Free Negroes Unlawfully Held in Bondage, the first organization whose mission was to abolish slavery.

Like Franklin, Pennsylvania also took the lead in antislavery efforts. In 1780, Pennsylvania passed the Gradual Abolition Act, which stated that slaves born in Pennsylvania in 1780 or later would be legally freed by their twenty-eighth birthday. All other slaves who had moved into the city needed to be registered with

ERICA ARMSTRONG DUNBAR and KATHLEEN VAN CLEVE

the city government so that when they reached their twenty eighth birthday, they too would be freed.

Resolving the issue of slavery in the United States became one of Benjamin Franklin's final missions. Near the end of Franklin's life—and around when Ona walked along Philadelphia's cobblestone streets for the first time—Franklin did something that his younger self would have thought insane. He presented a petition to the new United States Congress for the abolishment of slavery, calling slavery "an atrocious debasement of human nature."

Clearly the man had changed his mind.

Ordinarily it would have made sense for the wife of the new president to visit this famous man. George Washington obviously knew Benjamin Franklin; it would have been impossible for him not to know Franklin. Despite this, Franklin was probably not anywhere on Martha's need-to-see list. She did not want to pretend to share common ground with Franklin or any other abolitionist. She had no intention of releasing her slaves, and in fact would do everything in her power to shield Ona and the rest of her slaves from the contagion of liberty that seemed to be spreading throughout Philadelphia.

It turns out that Martha did not do enough. Or perhaps, because she always surrounded herself with people who thought as she did, she didn't realize the size of her opposition. Besides conflicting with Benjamin Franklin's stance, Martha's stance on slavery collided directly with the practices of Philadelphia's foundational religion: Quakerism.

The colony of Pennsylvania had been founded by William Penn in 1681. Penn and many of the people who'd come with him had been Quakers, members of a Christian religious group called the Society of Friends. They believed in the "light of God" within every person, not just within priests or popes or important men in the church. (Indeed, equality between the sexes was always a basic guideline for Quakers.)

The Quakers (also called Friends) believed, among other things, in peace, equality, and simplicity, and they were wholly opposed to treating any person (even a king or a president) as superior to any other.

When the colony of Pennsylvania was established in the late seventeenth century, Quakers, like many other European landowners in the colonies, owned slaves. They thought it was okay because they believed that they treated their slaves humanely. It wasn't okay, and Quakers soon admitted this. A little less than a hundred years before Ona's birth, in 1688, a number of Quakers in Germantown, Pennsylvania (about eight miles away from Independence Hall), declared that slavery itself went against Quaker ideals of equality. It was a bold statement and had consequences: many of these Germantown Quakers were bullied and financially sabotaged for their declaration.

But the moral misgivings persisted. In 1711 Quakers from Chester County, Pennsylvania (about twenty miles from Philadelphia), asked the members of their congregation to stop purchasing new slaves. Further, they went on record to suggest that all Friends withdraw from the slave trade. By 1758 all Quakers in Pennsylvania forbade their members from owning slaves or otherwise participating in the slave trade.

By the time Martha and her procession arrived, the Quakers were speaking constantly to anyone, anywhere, about the evils of slavery. But it wasn't only the Quakers. There were people besides Quakers and black men and women who opposed slavery in Philadelphia. Matthew Carey, an Irish-born Catholic, was one of them.

At the time, one way people received information—news, weather, politics—was through a printed document similar to a newspaper page. (Remember, this was two hundred years before computers.) To reach as many people as possible, particularly about an important event, printers would make copies of a "broadside," a document that could be plastered all over the broad side of a wall. Similar to the huge movie posters at bus stops or other large advertisements that are created today, people would have a hard time not seeing them.

Carey was a printer who had once worked for Benjamin Franklin. In 1789 Carey reprinted a famous broadside that had come to the United States from London. It was called *Description of a Slave Ship*, and its publication marked one of the first times that the people of both Great Britain and the United States could actually learn for themselves what it meant to transport thousands of Africans to the shores of the Americas.

The broadside showed everyone that the slave trade was brutal and completely inhumane. Illustrations of the ship above the text showed Africans packed together as tightly as possible, with no attention paid to space or cleanliness or hunger or dignity. When the broadside was printed in Philadelphia, it gave the Quakers and all the other abolitionists—as well as anyone who did not yet hold an opinion about the enslavement of humans—an image of such suffering and pain that the movement to end slavery in Pennsylvania was given a huge shove forward.

When Martha and Robert Lewis and Ona and the rest of them arrived in Philadelphia in May 1789, the

ERICA ARMSTRONG DUNBAR and KATHLEEN VAN CLEVE

broadside was *everywhere*. Everyone was talking about it—people would shout from the streets that slavery was a disgrace, that it was an abomination. Even at the stylish places where Martha went—the stores, the gardens, the homes—the broadside was visible. Martha would have had to turn her face and force her eyes to connect with something that did not bring up such a personally disruptive subject.

Wherever Martha went, Ona went. When Martha turned her head to avoid the broadside, Ona would have seen it. Even though she couldn't read or write, the picture would have startled her. She would not have had time to study it, because Martha would have been on the move. Still, as Ona walked behind Martha's carriage along the twenty blocks from Gray's Ferry to the Morrises' home, she would have been struck by a realization so strong that it was like the force that cracked Philadelphia's own Liberty Bell.

There she was: wearing her best dress, her hair neatly combed, behind the carriage of the wife of the president, a little comfortable, perhaps a little proud in the knowledge that she was one of Martha Washington's personal slaves and not, for example, stuck in a wheat field or shackled inside a slave ship. But then she may have looked around. Some people may have been staring at her—black people. Perhaps she caught the eyes of someone and recognized him as a free black man. Next to him, possibly, was a free black woman. And next to them, more free black people. None of them would have seemed impressed by her. Instead they would have seemed bothered, and offended.

Think about moments when a new discovery may have turned your head upside down about the nature of things and then think about how Ona may have felt when she met free black men and women in Philadelphia. She would have realized that pride in working for the president and his wife was also a cloud that kept her from seeing what was obvious to free black men and women—that her pride needed to be replaced with fury.

So much was new. So much was strange. And now she was confronted with the fact that some black people in this northern state did not think the way her family did—that it was possible to live only the way she and her family had always lived at Mount Vernon: in bondage from birth until death.

Ona would not know yet that there were successful black professionals living freely and relatively happily in the new United States, such as the astronomer Benjamin Banneker or the poet Jupiter Hammon. That was coming. Yet even without knowing, Ona would have felt the rumblings of discontent, the sense that her life as she knew it was based on flawed understandings. The bitter fact that she was enslaved did not change the better fact that her mind was free to think as she chose. In this spirit, Ona entered Philadelphia with a locked sense of how the world *was* and left Philadelphia with a sense of how it *could be*, even for her.

CHAPTER SEVEN
NEW YORK

ONA WAS IN PHILADELPHIA FOR FIVE DAYS. SHE WORKED nonstop. Martha liked to see her old friends, go shopping, and enjoy good meals, and it was Ona's job to shadow Martha, making herself metaphorically invisible unless there was a problem. Martha had a grand time. She later wrote to her niece, Fanny Bassett, that she loved her time in Philadelphia and that her granddaughter Nelly had become friends with young Maria Morris, the daughter of her hostess, Mary Morris. Robert Morris, Mary's husband, had already left Philadelphia and was going to meet the group in Elizabethtown, New Jersey, later that week.

It took two days for the procession to reach

Elizabethtown, where there was a formal dock for boats crossing the Hudson River. When Martha and her procession arrived, Robert Morris and the president were there to greet them. At the dock was a forty-seven-foot-long barge waiting to take them across the Hudson River to their new home. This was the same barge that George had taken a month earlier to New York—one that had been built in honor of the new president. Thirteen rowers waited for Martha and the grandchildren to board the barge, all of the rowers wearing perfectly matched black hats and white shirts. Ona, the rest of the slaves, the horses, and the baggage would not go on the presidential barge. They would follow in a ferryboat.

Ona would have been able to stand against the railing on the ferry as she crossed the river. This would be another world-expanding experience—she would have been able to see the crowds gathered around what is now known as the Battery at the southern tip of Manhattan; she could watch as the soldiers triggered the thirteen-gun salute to honor the president and his family. If Martha had been treated like a celebrity in Baltimore and Philadelphia, George was an absolute rock star in New York City. When the ferry docked at Peck's Slip, Ona would have gazed at the jumble of brick buildings standing tall in front of her. As in

Philadelphia, the buildings would have been squashed next to one another alongside paved or cobblestoned roads with whale-oil streetlamps lining the sidewalks. After New York governor George Clinton gave a speech, the Washingtons and their fellow passengers were led immediately to the mansion on Cherry Street. Ona's eyes would have been darting left and right, up and down. Another city, another shock to her sense of the world.

Ona did not see the Empire State Building. It didn't exist yet. At the end of the eighteenth century, there were no skyscrapers, no subways, no taxis or Uber, and no Central Park in New York City. Most of the residents lived downtown, south of Thirty-Fourth Street. Unlike Mount Vernon—the massive estate where the manor house spread out like a Death Star among the various slave cabins, assorted vocational buildings, and vast farmland—downtown New York City was one bustling, hustling, aggressive swarm of human activity.

People were *everywhere*. Ona would have had to step aside to let people by her, and then she'd have to jump back to where she'd been so that she wouldn't get pushed by someone else. Wagons and carts would have filled the streets next to fancy carriages and sleek horses, led by New York–based black postilions, like the Washington slaves Giles and Paris. New York City was not like Philadelphia; slaves were still acceptable in this metropolis. In fact, it was a status symbol for the rich to have enslaved black postilions. For Martha, this was a bonus; she did not have to put up her guard like she had in Philadelphia with people who thought more like Benjamin Franklin than George Clinton, New York's slave-owning governor.

In the same way that the thirteen states had inconsistent currencies, they also had inconsistent laws about slavery. Pennsylvania—and especially Philadelphia—was a leader in the battle to abolish slavery, but it was not alone. Massachusetts (which included Maine at the time) and Connecticut had also outlawed slaves. New Hampshire (which included Vermont at the time) had greatly decreased its number of slaves. Other states—such as New York and New Jersey—were much more protective of their slave owners. It was a time of instability—a chronological crossroads when someone like New York governor George Clinton could be a member of New York's abolitionist society *and* own slaves. As usual with instability at the top, the effect trickled down in a miserable way to black residents living in New York City in 1789. If you were a free black person, you most likely lived in poverty. If you were an enslaved black person, you were, well, enslaved.

One of the major differences in slavery between

the northern and southern states was that there were no massive plantations in the North. (Yes, there were farms—big farms on Long Island and in the Pine Barrens of New Jersey and on Cape Cod in Massachusetts—but none of them had the scope of the tobacco and rice and wheat plantations of the South.) In a city like New York, space itself was limited. This meant that the majority of whites who owned slaves in New York did not own a great number of them.

Ona would have been even more surprised that in New York there were more enslaved black women than men. In this part of the country, keeping a household running was the priority. This work was often completed by women. Think of how much needs to be done in your own home by your own family to keep everyone fed, clothed, and healthy. Then remember that in Ona's time there were no dishwashers or refrigerators or washing machines.

In order to have hot water, servants and slaves—usually women—had to first go to a well in the backyard, then carry heavy barrels of water back to the house, transfer the water to cast iron pots, and heat those pots over a fire. In order to scrub clothes, they would have to make their own soap. As part of cleaning the house, they would have to pick up the rugs and beat them with a rod. The houses of rich New

ERICA ARMSTRONG DUNBAR and KATHLEEN VAN CLEVE

Yorkers were often filled with people; George and Martha's house would not be any different. There were going to be about thirty people living underneath the one roof at 3 Cherry Street, the house downtown on Manhattan Island where the Washingtons would live. The work would seem endless.

While Ona, like all slaves, was expected to work all the time, her focus would be on Martha—not the house. The people who had to do much of the domestic work were some of the enslaved black men as well as most of the fourteen white servants who needed to be hired in order to get all the work done.

Ona had lived around white people—that is, her owners—for all her life. But she was not accustomed to living daily in the same house with white servants, even considering the times that Ona would have stayed with Martha in the mansion house when so ordered. She hadn't spent much time with white people who were desperately poor, struggling, and powerless. But standing alongside white servants, Ona would see even more clearly the distinction between their lives and hers. To be a slave—even the favored slave of the wife of the president of the United States—was to be seen as inhuman. To be free was to be given your humanity back. This would have been a recognition so powerful that we can almost see Ona as she slowly begins to raise her head and look around at her new home, her new city, her new work colleagues.

It would have made perfect sense if Ona had flashed back to the memory of the black men and women living and working freely in Philadelphia. As she stood on the threshold of this new home, with its wooden door and marble steps, Ona would have been aware that she was the property of the Washingtons. In this conflicted state of New York, Ona may have seen her future with brighter, sharper eyes. Life would be different here in the North. She would be different too.

ERICA ARMSTRONG DUNBAR and KATHLEEN VAN CLEVE

CHAPTER EIGHT

SURVIVING

IN MANY WAYS NEW YORK CITY IN 1789 HAD THE SAME definable characteristic it does today: it was a city so encompassing that within it was the best of everything and the worst of everything. Back then this characteristic meant that it was hard to figure out what to trust, what to expect, what to value. Just like a young child learning a new language—the words, the meanings, the rules—the United States needed to learn the meanings and rules of a Constitution that said everyone was born equal and deserving of the same rights, while upholding a system where some humans were definitely not equal and did not have the same rights. It was going to take a long time. Meanwhile, New

York City, out of all the cities in the new country, was the most glaring example of what happened when a new country hadn't figured things out yet.

It had rich residents like Governor Clinton; it had the desperately poor, like some of the white servants coming to work for the Washingtons. It had the educated classes—people like Aaron Burr, the future vice president, who had graduated from Princeton; and Alexander Hamilton, the future secretary of the treasury and founder of the *New York Post*, who had graduated from King's College (now called Columbia University). And it had people (even besides the enslaved) who had never gone to school, not even for a day. It had abolitionists who were part of the New York Manumission Society—("manumission" is what happens when a slave owner frees his slaves)—but many of these abolitionists were (yes) slave owners.

Escaped slaves hid in the busy city's dark corners and alleyways, hopeful for a job where their identity would not be discovered. Free blacks worked any jobs they could get, which were not many. Social-climbing rich white people owned slaves to make them feel more important and to benefit from their labor. Many free black men and women lived proudly and publicly, even forming their own clubs and organizations that fought for the reputation and credibility of the blacks who

ERICA ARMSTRONG DUNBAR and KATHLEEN VAN CLEVE

lived in New York City. Everything was in upheaval—the laws, the customs, even the location for the new federal government. Over the next eighteen months, life as Ona knew it would be thrown up into the air and juggled. It would not settle into a routine again for many, many months.

On her first day in New York City, Martha Washington, fifty-eight years old, went straight to a dinner. Ona would have dressed her and fixed her hair—again—and made sure her shoes did not have any clumps of dirt on their heels and that her corset was suitably tight. She may have accompanied her owner to the dinner even though Ona (if not Martha) was probably exhausted. One of the reasons why Martha was able to engage in so many social activities, besides her innate energy, was Ona. Like a thermometer permanently set on "calm," Ona was the constant mood regulator for Martha, who was allowed to act however she wanted—to be sad, to be angry, to snap at someone, to be cool and icy, to be exuberant. Ona was there to help Martha on whatever ruffled emotional ocean she was traveling. (This was what differentiated Ona from someone like her sister-in-law, Charlotte, who could not stop herself from lashing out at the estate manager and at slavery in general.) Ona's ability not to lose her cool—along with her intelligence and bravery—would become even more important to Martha in the days ahead.

In June 1789, not even a month after Martha arrived in New York, a potential calamity struck. George Washington, fifty-seven, became very sick.

In some ways, it was strange that he hadn't gotten ill earlier. This was a world where the average life span was between thirty-five and forty-five years old. George had been a soldier for most of his adult life. Difficult and often unclean conditions at war, as well his advancing age, had taken their toll on George's body. When he came down with a fever in June, it didn't go away. Instead it lasted, and with it, a tumor grew on his left leg. Soon he was in such pain that he could not move. By June 17 the well-respected New York doctor Samuel Bard had no choice but to operate on the president's leg.

It was a nerve-racking time for everyone inside the house, and undoubtedly for those people aware of his sickness on the outside. The beginning of anything brings anxiety; the beginning of the United States was no different. George Washington was the president whom everyone seemed to want to be in charge, and for him not to survive would have been seen as catastrophic. The household decided to keep his sickness a secret, and this made a terrible situation even worse.

The first president of the United States was seriously ill, and having to keep up the pretense that he was healthy was difficult for everyone who lived with him, Ona included.

Martha was already unhappy to be in New York. To be there with a sick husband triggered every one of her anxieties. Her reliance on Ona intensified. Ona, plunged into the foreign world of the North, would have no opportunity to do anything but wait on Martha, who was waiting on George. Throughout the next several months, it was unclear whether he would survive.

At first the household had no idea what to do. Yet life did go on. There were clothes to be sewn and hair to be combed and grandchildren who needed activities and schooling. Food supplies needed to be obtained from the nearest market. Shoes had to be fixed. In New York it was not as easy as sending the shoes to the shoemaker, or going to the grist-mill to get flour. All these kinds of supplies needed to be purchased and carried and sorted. The slaves and servants had to figure this out in the unfamiliar, confusing, busy hive of activity known as New York City. And as usual, they did.

George survived because of a combination of good medical care, his natural good health, and, most of all, sheer luck. Still, it took him a long time to recover—the entire fall and much of the winter. It wasn't until February 1790 that he was able to resume his presidential schedule.

It's hard to imagine Ona's confusion during her first winter in the North. New York snowfalls can be brutally cold, even dangerous. She undoubtedly slipped on the slick cobblestones, iced over by freezing rain. She certainly shivered when she found herself outside without a warm-enough coat. And she unquestionably felt the cold wind through the window sashes of the bedroom she shared with Moll, way up in the attic on Cherry Street. Maybe she discovered that one of the good things about the house being so crowded was that it helped to warm things up during the winter.

As George grew stronger, Martha resumed the whirlwind of New York life. Very few people, besides Ona and George, knew Martha's true feelings. She served, and served well, as the president's social partner, an ideal image of grace and respectability. Unlike George, who was not comfortable socializing with strangers, Martha would open the house on Cherry Street to her female friends and acquaintances at seven o'clock in the evening, serving tea, coffee, lemonade, and ice cream. These evenings could go on until ten o'clock. On Thursdays, as George continued to get better, he and Martha began to host formal dinners that had to include people from all walks of political life. Foreign ministers, senators, and congressmen, as well as Cabinet members, were invited to dine, and it was Martha who had to keep the conversation moving and upbeat.

Ona would have looked forward to the Washingtons' social occasions, as it would have given her a chance to be by herself. At Mount Vernon she would have been able to escape at night to the Quarters to be with her mother and her siblings. In New York this was not an option; she was always surrounded by people.

When George had fully recovered, the household moved to a bigger home nearby, at 39–41 Broadway. This house had views of the Hudson River, fine carpets, and beautiful furniture. Of course, the burden of moving—remember, this was before moving vans and dollies and U-Haul—fell on the slaves. It is hard to think about Ona, her full skirts tangling up her every move, carrying heavy crates downstairs and upstairs.

Once they were in the new house, Ona probably tried again to settle into a routine: in the morning, perhaps escorting Nelly to Mrs. Graham's School on Maiden Lane, the same street where Thomas Jefferson lived. In the afternoon, sewing and cleaning Martha's dresses. At night, preparing Martha for whatever social event she had planned. Ona would have learned the streets of downtown Manhattan in this way, even coming to recognize some of the people who crossed her path. Perhaps there was a young free black man who tipped his hat to her. Perhaps she walked by the African Free School for black children that had been created by the New York Manumission Society. This school ended up educating most of the black men who became well-known leaders during the 1800s—men including Alexander Crummell, Henry Highland Garnet, and James McCune Smith, among others. Ona still could not read or write, but she was observing, listening, and remembering—exactly what students were supposed to be doing at all the New York schools.

In June 1790, Ona may have picked up Nelly on Maiden Lane very close to the time when a famous dinner took place at Thomas Jefferson's house. The dinner was not only famous because of the people who were there: Jefferson, Alexander Hamilton, and James Madison. It was famous—indeed legendary—because of the consequences it had for the new country, the politicians representing the country, and the slaves who were not yet allowed to claim the country for themselves. Alexander Hamilton wanted the

ERICA ARMSTRONG DUNBAR and KATHLEEN VAN CLEVE

capital of the United States to remain in New York. Thomas Jefferson and James Madison, both from Virginia, wanted the capital to be on the Potomac River, near Mount Vernon.

Hamilton and Jefferson weren't fond of each other—but they also knew that they had to work together. Besides the location of the new country's capital, Hamilton's priority was the assumption of states' debts by the new federal government. (In other words, he wanted the federal government to pay the bills racked up by the individual states during the Revolutionary War.) Jefferson and Madison and most southern leaders did not want this to happen because (a) the southern states did not owe as much money as the northern states, because of slavery, and (b) they did not want to risk having the federal government grow more powerful than the states. Hamilton offered up a deal: the capital city could be on the Potomac if the federal government paid the debts.

Jefferson and Madison said yes. And as a kicker, they agreed that Philadelphia would be the temporary capital of the United States for the ten years it would take to build this new "Federal City" on the Potomac.

What did this have to do with Ona? Everything.

She had just moved from Mount Vernon to New York. Then she'd moved from Cherry Street to Broadway. The household had always been planning on going to Mount Vernon for the summer months. (She would have to pack for that too.) And now these founding fathers had thrown yet another wrench into her life. The only glimmer of hope for Ona was that she was going to return to Philadelphia, the place that offered many more opportunities to black people than were offered in New York or, certainly, in Virginia.

George Washington agreed with Thomas Jefferson and James Madison. He wanted the nation's capital to be on the Potomac. He would do anything to be closer to his beloved Mount Vernon. But before the Washingtons could go back for the summer, another medical scare occurred. After the move to their home on Broadway, George again became sick. Influenza— the flu—had recently spread throughout the city. Perhaps because of his long illness during the previous year, George was susceptible to this virus, and by late April he too was diagnosed with the deadly flu. This time people found out. Pennsylvania congressman George Clymer wrote, "But it is observed here with a great deal of anxiety that his general health seems to be declining."

Hundreds of New Yorkers died, young and old.

ERICA ARMSTRONG DUNBAR and KATHLEEN VAN CLEVE

George Washington was not one of them. He lost much of his hearing, but he survived.

The summer move back to Mount Vernon had been postponed. Now, finally, in August 1790, the Washingtons were able to leave New York for Virginia. Everyone, from the president to Ona, was eager to take a step back from this very tumultuous life in the city. In one year Ona had experienced more change and upheaval than many people do in a lifetime, and she did it all as a young teenager serving the most powerful couple in the country.

When Ona returned to Mount Vernon and hugged her mother, Betty, she would do so with the wiser eyes of someone who had seen much that could not be easily explained. And when she moved to Philadelphia in the fall, she would be wiser still.

CHAPTER NINE

THE PRESIDENT'S HOUSE

PHILADELPHIANS WEREN'T VERY HAPPY THAT THEIR CITY was not going to be the capital of the new country. Some of them were sure that if they could just prove to George Washington and other powerful members of Congress how perfect Philadelphia was during their time in the city, the government officials would change their minds and stay.

This was never going to happen. First and foremost, George Washington identified as a Virginian. No matter how much he may have enjoyed his time in various northern states, and no matter how much he respected some of his northern colleagues, he was adamant about having the capital be located near his home at Mount

Vernon—not just for his lifetime but for postcrity.

The builders called the new capital the Federal City. (It would be named Washington, District of Columbia, for George Washington himself after his death and when it was finished being built.) In the spirit of a brand-new country, this would be a brand-new city, built on the Potomac River, where only a few of the visionary city planners could see past the swamps and mosquitoes to the beautiful city that was to come.

Because it was built in the South, the actual men and women who cleared the land and laid the bricks and cut the lumber were the same resourceful and hard-working labor force who had made the economy of the South so profitable: the enslaved. In fact, it was an element of the compromise among Jefferson, Madison, and Hamilton that the slaves who would be working under the hot sun of northern Virginia were going to be rented from slave owners in the South. The majority of them would never be paid for their work.

Meanwhile, Ona and the other slaves returned to their home at Mount Vernon that August 1790 with all the delight and misgivings of anyone who returns home after a year away in a very different place. Ona would have been happy to see her mother as well as her siblings (which included a brother Tom and a sister Philadelphia).

She would also learn that her older sister, Betty Davis, had given birth to a little girl named Nancy. What would have been the hardest part for Ona—after she embraced her mother and cradled her niece—was the fact that she had returned to Mount Vernon a different person from the young girl who had left more than a year earlier. How could she explain to her family what it was like to live in New York City, with the Washingtons, their political aides, their servants, and the enslaved all spilling out of shared rooms? How could she tell them what it was like to live in a city where some of the black residents were not owned by white people? Would they even believe her? How could she describe Philadelphia and the free black men and women in the markets, and the talk everywhere about black freedom?

While she understood that some slaves at Mount Vernon looked at her with envy because she was Martha's favored attendant, she now had seen for herself that there were black people who lived without being anyone's slave, favored or not. This must have made her gaze at baby Nancy with intense hope and equally vivid longing, both for her niece and for herself.

There is some evidence that during his life George Washington questioned the morality of slavery. However, there is conclusive proof that George and Martha did not let the question of immorality get in the way of

ERICA ARMSTRONG DUNBAR and KATHLEEN VAN CLEVE

bringing their favored slaves to Philadelphia when they moved in 1790. What the Washingtons had learned about slave owning in New York was not that owning humans was inhumane (as Benjamin Franklin believed) but that they needed to be even more careful about which slaves would accompany them to their new home. (Benjamin Franklin would not be in Philadelphia when the Washingtons arrived in November. He died at the age of eighty-four in April 1790, after he'd petitioned Congress one last time about the inhumanity of people owning other people.)

Giles, Paris, Christopher Sheels, Austin, Ona, and Moll had all earned the Washingtons' trust and would return. William Lee was now too old, too injured, and too unhelpful to go back north. George ordered that he be cared for at Mount Vernon. (In George's will, William Lee was provided with a yearly amount of thirty dollars for the rest of his life, and he was the only slave of George's who was immediately freed.)

George was also adding two people from Mount Vernon, a father and son. Richmond was a seventeen-year-old who had not yet shown any specific skill. His father, however, was someone who had become quite well known and respected among the slaves and white people at Mount Vernon. This was the Washingtons' spectacular chef, Hercules, a vain, strict, imperious slave who ran his kitchen with supreme authority. When he asked his staff to do something, "his underlings flew in all directions" trying desperately to please this man who was not pleased easily. Hercules was an impressive-looking person; he was handsome, and appearances mattered to him, just like they did to George. That is probably another reason why the president wanted Hercules to come with him to Philadelphia.

Hercules knew what kinds of food George liked and could eat—usually something mushy, because George always had dental problems. (George's favorite breakfast? Hoecakes—a kind of pancake made with corn flour and smothered in butter and honey to make it soft and sweet enough to eat.) But Hercules could also put on a lavish banquet when it was necessary. The amount of food at Hercules's command was extraordinary: for one week in 1794, the chef had to manage almost three hundred pounds of beef, one hundred thirty pounds of lamb, forty-four chickens, and twenty-two pigeons, among many other ingredients. He had been purchased by George in 1767 as a thirteen-year-old ferryman; he'd learned how to cook at Mount Vernon from the Washingtons' previous chef-slave, a woman called Doll. Despite being bossy in the kitchen, Hercules was always careful to seem deferential to George and Martha themselves. The Washingtons wholeheartedly believed they could trust him.

ERICA ARMSTRONG DUNBAR and KATHLEEN VAN CLEVE

The caravan left Mount Vernon in November 1790 and headed straight to Sixth and Market Streets in Philadelphia. This was the home of Robert and Mary Morris, the same couple who had welcomed Martha eighteen months earlier. Their house was less than six hundred feet from Independence Hall, the site at which George and the other founding fathers had signed the Constitution of the United States (and before that, the Declaration of Independence, even though George himself had already been fighting the war). The Morrises had moved out in order for George and Martha to move in. From now on, and continuing through the presidential terms of John Adams, this home was known as the President's House.

The building was one of the largest homes in the city. Originally built between 1767 and 1768, it had already served three families besides the Morrises. One of them was that of Benedict Arnold, the most famous traitor from the American Revolution. Like the mansion in New York City, every inch of the President's House would be used to accommodate the twenty-five to thirty people who would be living in it year-round. Like many other colonial city homes of the rich and powerful, the President's House was three stories tall and the width of two city row houses. While undoubtedly big for the city, it was smaller than the Washingtons' home on Broadway in New York and just a fraction of the size of Mount Vernon. It had marble steps and mahogany doors, fancy couches and impressive fireplaces.

Just as in New York, Ona would live here with white and black people. George Washington's personal secretary, Tobias Lear, would live there with his wife, Polly, and their toddler, Benjamin. Four other aides to the president would live there as well: Howell Lewis, Bartholomew Dandridge, Robert Lewis, and Major William Jackson. The first three were George's nephews. Major Jackson had served alongside George during the war. Rounding out the living quarters would be the fifteen additional white servants whom Tobias Lear was forced to hire in order to run the household without disruption.

Ona would spend the next six years living in a house that numbered between twenty-five and thirty residents. Privacy would be rare for George and Martha; for Ona and the other slaves, it was basically impossible. This was especially true for Ona: her bedroom would share a door with George and Martha's bedroom on the second floor.

The house had recently been configured to include bedrooms for the grandchildren, so on one side of the Washingtons' bedroom was a room for Nelly, who would share it with the slave Moll. On the other side was a room

ERICA ARMSTRONG DUNBAR and KATHLEEN VAN CLEVE

for Washy, who was sharing it with Ona. It is hard to imagine Ona becoming comfortable with sleeping in a room that shared a door with the bedroom of the president and his wife. It is a sad fact of slavery that many times enslaved women and girls had to constantly be prepared for assaults by white men, confrontations that usually left them desperately aware that both a smaller physical size and their status as property kept them powerless. This was true for every enslaved woman, Moll and Ona included.

The house would be filled to the rooftop with people all the time. There was, however, a surprising benefit to this—at least for Ona. Every day she could examine the lives of the free white servants from Philadelphia. She could watch as these servants received pay for their work, moved about the city as they wished, and made decisions about their lives, including quitting their jobs if they desired.

As she folded Washy's clothes and escorted Martha out through the imposing mahogany doors, Ona would have passed by the servants in the hallway, in the kitchen, everywhere. We can almost see her as she carefully studied the habits and choices of her white companions. She would have noticed that they did not ask permission for anything. And she would have begun thinking about a life where she did not have to ask for it either.

CHAPTER TEN

THE GRADUAL ABOLITION ACT

ONA WAS NOT THE ONLY ENSLAVED PERSON PAYING attention. Three enslaved people claimed their freedom in Philadelphia on April 6, 1791, after they had learned about Pennsylvania's Gradual Abolition Act. Their actions would have a direct effect on how Ona Judge and the other Washington slaves were treated by the president and his wife.

The Gradual Abolition Act had been passed into law in 1780. Pennsylvania had taken the lead in antislavery legislation with the passage of this law, but it was complicated. Many Pennsylvanians felt as if they could not end slavery in one fell swoop but instead needed to be very clear about the process by which the enslaved could claim their freedom. The law stated:

- No one could import new slaves into Pennsylvania.
- Slave owners in Pennsylvania had to register their slaves at the local courthouse.
- If children were born to enslaved Pennsylvania mothers, their legal status would be "indentured servant" instead of "slave," and they would have to work for their mother's owner until age twenty-eight.
- If an enslaved person was brought to Pennsylvania by a slave owner from another state, the enslaved person would be freed if they remained in Pennsylvania for longer than six months.
- Slave owners who were members of Congress did not have to abide by this law.

The three slaves who claimed their freedom were owned by another founding father of America, although he wasn't as famous as George Washington. He had not believed that his slaves would be smart enough or aware enough to learn about the Gradual Abolition Act. He had also thought that they might have preferred living as slaves, which sounds unbelievable, but it was a justification for slavery that many slave owners believed at the time. In any event, the slave owner was caught completely off guard when his slaves came to him and told him, politely, that they were choosing freedom.

The most embarrassing part of the situation was that this slave owner was someone who should have known the laws backward and forward. His name was Edmund Randolph, and he was the chief lawyer—or attorney general—of the new United States. Randolph was the guy to thank for the idea of a legislative branch of the federal government that is made up of two parts: the House of Representatives and the Senate. He had been an aide to George during the Revolutionary War and, later on, the governor of Virginia. In 1791 Randolph thought he could keep his slaves because he was a federal official—but he was wrong. Only members of Congress were allowed to keep their slaves. The act said nothing about federal officials. More important, Randolph had badly underestimated his slaves. He had not realized that the allure of freedom was so bright that enslaved people, helped out by the free black community in Philadelphia, would do anything they could to find their way to it.

Randolph could do nothing to stop his slaves from leaving him. That was done. But he could stop a similar situation from happening to his friends—especially

ERICA ARMSTRONG DUNBAR and KATHLEEN VAN CLEVE

the president and his wife. He immediately visited the President's House, insistent that he talk to George. But the president was not in Philadelphia. He was in Virginia as part of his three-month tour of the southern states. Randolph then asked to speak to Martha. For sure, Randolph had been at the President's House before, on many occasions, and each time Ona was undoubtedly by Martha's side. This day would be different. The situation was delicate, Randolph may have explained, perhaps avoiding Ona's eyes. He needed to have a *private* conversation with Martha. Probably his eyes glanced quickly at Ona, and Martha immediately understood. She dismissed Ona from the room.

Ona would have been curious, of course, since it was very rare for Martha to give her time alone. Yet she would have obeyed. Maybe she went outside and took a deep breath of the fresh April air. Maybe she closed her eyes and imagined her mother, Betty, at Mount Vernon. Maybe she thought about the new black church that was forming just a few blocks away.

Maybe she had already heard through the lightning-fast grapevine of black Philadelphia that Randolph's slaves were claiming their freedom, and maybe she was wondering what it would be like for her, too, to leave the only owners she had ever known.

If Ona had been thinking about this, she and Attorney

General Randolph would have been on the same wavelength. Edmund Randolph had come to the President's House to tell George and Martha not to make the same mistake he had. He had spent the day examining all the laws. He was legally unable to get his slaves back. The truth was, Randolph had completely misjudged the abolition laws in the northern states. Like many southerners, including George Washington, he had told himself that the institution of slavery was actually helpful to the slaves—that enslaved men and women were better off with a generous owner, that they were well fed, sheltered, and cared for. In fact, many of these same southern white men and women would have said that they treated their slaves almost as though they were members of the family.

This kind of thinking is sometimes called "paternalism," a belief that an authority can protect people by giving them what they need to survive, but those people are not given any responsibility or freedom to make their own choices. With respect to slavery, the belief that the slaves should be content with their position in life was widespread among white slave owners, many of whom also believed that they were treating the enslaved with privilege and special care. (George and Martha certainly believed this.) It seems obvious today that slavery was inhumane, but at the time, it was easier for slave owners to believe they were doing the slaves a favor by clothing them and giving them shelter, rather than the slave owners trying to imagine living in the slaves' shoes for even one second.

What was equally absurd was that slave owners such as the Washingtons and Edmund Randolph thought that their slaves were incapable of learning and understanding the laws of the land. This was part of a self-fulfilling prophecy. Since the majority of slave owners did not allow slaves to learn how to read or write, it would be hard for slaves to learn and understand the laws of the land. It had not occurred to Randolph that in moving to Philadelphia, his slaves would be exposed to free people who would teach them what Randolph would not. He warned Martha that she and George must pay attention to their own slaves: "Those who were of age in this family might follow the example, after a residence of six months should put it in their power."

Ona and Christopher, Paris and Giles, Hercules and Richmond, Austin and Moll—all of them, potentially, could leave the Washingtons' household under the Pennsylvania law. Martha took this very seriously. She met with Tobias Lear, George's secretary, who wrote George a letter explaining the Randolph situation. It would be a terrible thing for their own slaves to learn about the law and leave, not to mention how embarrassing for the president and his wife if their slaves turned the laws against them.

Tobias wrote George a letter asking for him to "give directions in the matter respecting the blacks in the family." Tobias himself felt personally torn, not that he would have said that to George. He was from a town in New Hampshire called Portsmouth, which was an increasingly busy shipping port in the late eighteenth century. As with many of the northern states, slavery existed in New Hampshire, and while slavery had not been completely outlawed, there were only about 140 slaves and 630 free blacks living there. Tobias was George's "eyes and ears" on the ground in Philadelphia and was probably a bit more realistic than Randolph or Martha about the animosity toward slavery in the northern states. It would take all of Tobias's planning and all of George's reserve to keep this powder keg of antislavery forces from blowing up in his face.

This was even more difficult than expected. George Washington—despite his many achievements—was almost always in debt. His harvests never earned him as much money as he needed to pay off his bills. The truth was that Martha was much "richer" than George—or at least Martha's family was richer. The property that George controlled after their marriage was still owned by Martha and the Custis family (the heirs of her first husband). In this case, slaves equaled property, and property equaled money. If Ona and the

ERICA ARMSTRONG DUNBAR and KATHLEEN VAN CLEVE

rest of the Washingtons' slaves claimed their freedom in Philadelphia, George would have to pay the estate of Martha's dead husband for the value of every slave that was gone. This was a lot of money in this era, and George did not have it.

George replied to Tobias Lear's letter very quickly. He blamed the increasingly bold abolitionists in Philadelphia for trying to wreck his lifestyle; these abolitionists made it their priority to find slaves like Ona so that they could tell her about the law in Pennsylvania. Despite his confidence that he treated his slaves well, he knew his slaves would be susceptible to the "epidemic" of black freedom. "For although I do not think they would be benefited by the change, yet the idea of freedom might be too great a temptation for them to resist."

Luckily, there was a loophole—a glaring space in the law that George and Martha believed would allow them to keep their slaves. They devised a simple, and deceptive, plan. If enslaved people were allowed to claim freedom after six months, then George and Martha (with Tobias Lear's help) would make sure that none of their slaves stayed in Pennsylvania one second longer than the six months. The slaves would be shuttled to and from Mount Vernon every six months, avoiding the stopwatch counting down to black freedom in Pennsylvania. If it was too inconvenient to get to Virginia from Philadelphia, a quick trip to a slave-owning state like New Jersey would serve the same purpose. The hourglass of slavery would be turned over every six months. The Washingtons' "property" would be safe.

Technically this was still illegal because of a 1788 amendment. Morally it was dishonest at best. The six-month clock existed for a reason that George chose to ignore. He must have known it was an underhanded practice, because he was very clear that his plan had to remain secret. He stated this plainly in his response to Tobias Lear: "I wish to have it accomplished under pretext that may deceive both them and the public. . . . This advice may be known to none but yourself and Mrs. Washington." It turns out that George Washington was just like all other humans: deeply flawed. Sometimes he was extremely decent; in this specific instance he acted in what he thought was his own personal best interest. Shuttling slaves in and out of Philadelphia before the end of a six-month timeline that would allow basic liberty to human beings was a terrible thing for George and Martha Washington to do. Moreover, it dishonored the man who had served the country so bravely, and so often at great personal risk. Yet both he and Martha had time to rectify their behavior—the question would be whether they would.

CHAPTER ELEVEN

A SIX-MONTH CLOCK

MARTHA WASHINGTON WAS A WOMAN WHO LOVED HER husband and her grandchildren. She was a strict domestic manager and kept track of the behavior and work patterns of all the slaves and servants. She was not interested in details of government or assumption of debts or the "enlightened" philosophical theories of the day. It appears that she did not spend any time thinking about the moral implications of slavery. Her goal was simple: keep her slaves in the dark about Pennsylvania's abolition laws.

Martha knew she had to act quickly. It was already April and the slaves' residency clock had started five months earlier in November 1790, when they'd arrived in Philadelphia. If the slaves found out about the law, they would know that in May they would be eligible for freedom. Given what Randolph had told Martha, it was just a matter of time before someone alerted the enslaved about the six-month residency provision.

Austin, Ona's brother, had actually arrived in Philadelphia at the end of October. His six-month clock was up, only he didn't know it. Martha came up with a sly plan to make sure that Austin would legally remain her property. She wrote a letter to her niece, Fanny Bassett Washington, who was back home at Mount Vernon, telling her that Austin was going to go "home" to see his friends and family even though she could barely "spare him at this time," but she wanted to fulfill her "promise to his wife."

Martha may have told Charlotte that Austin was coming home, but it was not because of a promise. She was just making up a story, knowing she would never be questioned about it. Indeed, the only person who could question her would be Austin, but he seems to have been too trusting of Martha to think that anything was strange about his abrupt trip to Mount Vernon. Or perhaps Austin knew about the Pennsylvania law but simply wanted to see his family. She gave him $11.66 for travel money—about $290 in today's dollars—and sent him on his way.

Now Martha could focus on the other slaves. She and George had recently discovered that they had misinterpreted one of the regulations of the Gradual Abolition Act. They originally thought that with respect to the teenage slaves—Christopher Sheels; Hercules's son, Richmond; and Ona—the Washingtons would not have to abide by the six-month clock. But Tobias Lear had discussed this with Edmund Randolph and found out that it wasn't true. Lear told the president that even these teenagers could claim freedom after six months.

The process of "claiming freedom" by teenagers was not an easy one. All of them would be required to be indentured servants until they were twenty-eight. But George and Martha seemed to have finally figured out that even this deterrent would not be enough to keep enslaved people from choosing freedom. George even wrote to Tobias that if his slaves found out they had a right to freedom, it would "make them insolent in a State of Slavery."

Tobias Lear agreed with George. There were many people in Philadelphia who would whisper the truth into the slaves' ears. "There were not wanting persons who would not only give them (the slaves) advice; but would use all means to entice them from their masters," Lear wrote to the president.

Once Martha confirmed that Austin had arrived

at Mount Vernon by April 24, she turned her attention to the rest of the slaves. There was no way for her to get the household moved to Mount Vernon by May 1. Instead she came up with another deceptive plan. New Jersey was a nearby state that did not outlaw slavery. She told Ona and Christopher Sheels that she needed to go to Trenton for a day. As soon as they took the ferry across the Delaware River, the Washingtons believed that Ona's and Christopher's six-month clocks would restart.

By now Giles and Paris were already with George on his tour around the southern states, so the Washingtons did not have to come up with another scheme to restart their freedom clocks. Richmond, Hercules's son, was scheduled to sail to Alexandria, Virginia, on April 25. This left Moll, the other enslaved woman charged with watching the Washington grandchildren in Philadelphia, and the famed domineering chef, Hercules.

Martha must have trusted Moll not to escape, because there were no plans for her to travel back to Mount Vernon. Hercules was another matter. "Uncle Harkless"—as Washy called him—was not a wide-eyed teenage slave. He was known throughout Philadelphia as a crucial member of the president's enslaved staff. Moreover, he had become kind of famous in his own

ERICA ARMSTRONG DUNBAR and KATHLEEN VAN CLEVE

right: Hercules was the kind of man who would walk around the city streets with a swagger. Part of this was because he was allowed to earn money. (The Washingtons allowed him to sell kitchen slops—leftover cooking items like tea leaves, animal skins, and soup broth. He often earned between one and two hundred dollars a year from these sales.) And while he may have saved some of this income, he also was not afraid to spend it on the latest male fashions. He bought a velvet-collared blue coat with shiny metal buttons, polished silver buckles for his shoes, and a pocket watch on a chain. He had a large network of friends in the free black community. Everyone knew who he was even if he wasn't brandishing the gold-headed cane that he liked to carry. It was not a stretch for anyone, least of all the Washingtons, to believe that if any of their slaves would learn about the law, it would be Hercules.

The Washingtons decided to play it cool. They casually asked Hercules if he would head back to Mount Vernon before the end of April. Hercules said yes. It did not seem to be a big deal.

But then it was. Someone—we don't know who— told Hercules about the Gradual Abolition Act. He immediately realized that the Washingtons' "casual" request had been nothing of the sort. They had asked him to go to Mount Vernon so that he wouldn't stay past six months in Philadelphia and be able to claim his freedom.

To Hercules the truth was instantly clear. After all his time and effort making splendid meals and running the kitchen like a magician, the Washingtons did not trust him. Hercules knew he had a decision to make. If he claimed his freedom, he would have to sacrifice his family—not only Richmond, his son, but his daughters, Evey and Delia, who were back at Mount Vernon. (Hercules's wife, Alice, had died four years earlier.) Hercules also knew that if he did choose his freedom, Evey, Delia, and Richmond might be punished.

This time Hercules chose his family. When Tobias Lear confronted Hercules, telling him that Tobias and the Washingtons knew that someone had told Hercules about the Gradual Abolition Act, Hercules put on a terrific show. He made sure to appear upset and desperate when he told Tobias that he had no intention of leaving the Washingtons. Tobias fell for it; he even wrote to the president, saying that Hercules "was mortified to the last degree to think that a suspicion could be entertained of his fidelity or attachment to you."

The Washingtons were pleased. Hercules had proven himself to be a loyal slave. They didn't have to worry about him anymore. Or so they thought.

ERICA ARMSTRONG DUNBAR and KATHLEEN VAN CLEVE

For the next five years, Hercules worked long and hard for the Washingtons. But then, in the summer of 1796, just after Ona escaped, something happened. Hercules was sent back to Mount Vernon. When the Washingtons returned to Philadelphia afterward, they took only two of their slaves. Hercules was not one of them. Further, he was "fired" as a chef and demoted to one of the worst jobs on the plantation—hard labor. He dug clay for bricks, spread dung, and smashed stones into sand so they could be used to plaster the exterior of buildings. It was a huge embarrassment for someone who had been as prominent as he'd been.

On February 22, 1797, Hercules ran away. It was George Washington's sixty-fifth birthday.

In 1791, however, Hercules was still trying to play by the rules of a world in which he had no legal say. But someone else, someone close to the Washingtons, was getting tired of playing by these rules. This was Tobias Lear, Washington's loyal secretary and a New Hampshire native.

Tobias had watched the Washingtons' treatment of the slaves with growing disappointment. He was a dedicated aide to George and Martha. He continued to be an accomplice for them in their slave shuffle. Yet right from the beginning, Tobias couldn't help voicing his own opinions about the slave trade to George

Washington, especially as he grew more impatient with the institution of slavery itself. He wrote in a letter to George Washington on April 24, 1791:

> *You will permit me now, Sir, (and I am sure you will pardon me for doing it) to declare that no consideration should induce me to take these steps to prolong the slavery of a human being, had I not the fullest confidence that they will at some future period be liberated, and the strongest conviction that their situation with you is far preferable to what they would probably obtain in a state of freedom.*

Tobias grew to be certain that freedom was the only moral choice for all Americans. He talked and wrote about this to George. George replied that he, too, was troubled by human bondage. He implied that he would—at some point—release his slaves into freedom. In the interim, Ona and the other slaves would move from Philadelphia to Mount Vernon and back, over and over again.

ERICA ARMSTRONG DUNBAR and KATHLEEN VAN CLEVE

CHAPTER TWELVE

A FREE BLACK COMMUNITY

THE TRUTH WAS THAT THE WASHINGTONS HAD NO REAL chance of keeping Ona and the other slaves ignorant of the changes in the country. Too much was going on. There had been a crack in the nation's soul as soon as the first abolitionist had spoken up about the immorality of slavery; by the time Ona moved to the President's House in Philadelphia, there was no way to stop the spread of the antislavery movement. At the same time, policy improvements—like the Gradual Abolition Act—did not mean that people's mind-sets changed. Racism was present; discrimination against people with darker skin remained as ugly and as common on the streets of Philadelphia as it was in Charleston,

South Carolina, or New York City. Slaves like Ona Judge had to constantly assess for themselves the risks of pursuing freedom against the known reality of their lives as property.

One of the people who knew this firsthand was the pastor Richard Allen, a free black man who lived in Philadelphia and who is rightly considered another founding father of America. Born enslaved and owned by Benjamin Chew, the chief justice of colonial Pennsylvania, Richard had been sold to another family in Delaware when he was still a child. There, his family had been split up—his mother and three siblings going to one white family and Richard going to another.

From sunup to sundown Richard worked in the wheat and flax fields of his owner, Stokeley Sturgis. From sundown to sunup, Richard would often be found listening to the sermons of traveling preachers, white and black. When he met a preacher named Freeborn Garrettson, perhaps in the late 1700s, Richard believed that he had received his own calling from God. He eventually adopted the teachings of the Methodist Church and its philosophy that charitable actions and hard work would improve one's life. Richard also believed that religion itself could form a bridge of understanding between races. If he could just prove to white people that slavery itself was

ERICA ARMSTRONG DUNBAR and KATHLEEN VAN CLEVE

not sanctioned by God and therefore was punishable during the afterlife, he was certain that most white people would decide it wasn't worth the trouble.

By 1780, Richard had made a deal with Sturgis to buy his freedom for two thousand dollars, and he made payments over the next five years. He paid off this debt early by working so hard at cutting wood that "it was only with difficulty I could open or close [my] hands."

By the time Ona moved to Philadelphia, Richard Allen was recognized as a leader of the free black community. In order to earn money, Richard transitioned from being a woodcutter to being a shoemaker (or cobbler) and a chimney sweep. In his free time, he was a preacher and a community leader. Today Richard is best known as the founder of Mother Bethel, a church on the corner of Sixth and Lombard Streets in Philadelphia whose formal name is the African Methodist Episcopal Church—or the AME Church. This church stands on the oldest parcel of ground continuously owned by black people. (Today the AME Church has almost 3.5 million members.) This was all due to Richard, who purchased the property after being forced too many times to sit in the balcony of the traditional white churches. The church became popular among the freed black communities.

In the 1800s Richard would become a bishop. In the 1790s he was leading the charge of freed, powerful, "modest but unafraid" black men and women.

The church was just seven blocks south of the President's House. Richard Allen himself lived at 150 Spruce Street, about four blocks away. Absalom Jones lived at 165 South Third Street, less than three blocks from the president's doorstep. Despite its size and status, Philadelphia was an eminently close-knit city. It would have been impossible for Ona not to have known about these influential free black leaders.

It would also have been impossible for her to talk to them, at least publicly. If the Washingtons knew she was communicating with free black leaders, they could banish Ona to Mount Vernon, or worse. Ona did not want to do anything to jeopardize her situation with the Washingtons, at least not yet. If and when she wanted to pursue freedom, it would be her decision. She was too aware of the nightmarish consequences that could happen. Freedom was still a faraway golden ring for Ona; she had only to look at the lives of three of her fellow enslaved Virginians from Mount Vernon.

Take Giles. He had been a loyal postilion for George Washington since the mid-1780s. During the spring of 1791, Giles was injured so severely that he was instantly returned to Mount Vernon. But he could not recover well enough to return to his old job. Instead, like Hercules after him, he was downgraded to the lowest possible position. The enslaved had to work even if they were injured, but now, instead of being the horseman for the president, he would have to make brooms or dig clay to make bricks.

Paris was another example, but in this case Paris showed Ona what would happen if she rebelled against the Washingtons directly. Paris had accompanied George on his three-month tour of the South (when Randolph had first told Martha about his slaves claiming freedom). But Paris had hit his limit. He was sick of having to pretend to be grateful for being a slave to the president. It showed. George wrote a letter to Tobias Lear describing Paris's behavior:

> Paris has become so lazy, self willed &
> impudent, that John (the Coachman)
> had no sort of government of him; on
> the contrary, John says it was a maxim
> with Paris to do nothing he was ordered,
> and every thing he was forbid.

Paris was ordered to return to Mount Vernon. He lived there two more years before he died of an illness. Christopher Sheels was also sent home to Mount

Vernon, with orders not to return to Philadelphia. Historians do not know why. It is possible that Christopher's ability to read and write had made the First Family uneasy. With the Washingtons' increasing need to keep their slaves in the dark about laws that could bring them freedom, Sheels would have been considered a threat.

The fact was that, despite the debate and despite the number of freed blacks in Philadelphia, slavery was so deeply rooted in the United States that it seemed unchangeable. George Washington himself got into the fray when he signed into law the Fugitive Slave Act in February 1793. According to this act, a slave owner (or someone acting on behalf of the slave owner) could legally capture a runaway slave and force him or her to appear in front of a judge. If the slave owner was able to provide written or oral "proof of ownership," the judge could order the return of the fugitive to the slave owner. The law also stated that anyone who helped a slave run away, or prevented the capture of a fugitive, would be imprisoned and fined five hundred dollars, and could be sued by the slave owner. (Five hundred dollars in 1793 was approximately the same as twelve thousand dollars today.)

Southerners were thrilled with this new law, especially because it was a federal decree, which meant that it didn't matter if a particular northern state had out-lawed slavery. This federal law overruled any state law. Many northerners were dismayed, if only because this law was a reminder of the growing divide in the country over the issue of slavery. This divide was reflected in the congressional vote for the law itself: it did not pass unanimously, another ominous sign that signaled the internal divisions in the country.

As a response to the Fugitive Slave Act, many northern states passed "personal liberty" laws requiring that any black person accused of being a fugitive slave was entitled to a trial with a jury. The personal liberty laws could also be used by northern states to accuse a slave owner or his agent of kidnapping an escaped slave if the recapture of the accused fugitive was not done through appropriate measures.

The right of all citizens to a trial by jury is the "due process" established in the Fifth Amendment to the US Constitution, which says that "no person shall . . . be deprived of life, liberty, or property, without due process of law." The southern states argued that the federal law protected their own property rights because in this case the property was a human being. In the end the fighting did not stop, and all potential runaway slaves were aware of how much danger they would be in if they chose to chase their freedom.

At this point Ona may not have been contemplating escape. But like most slaves, she had a constant fear of being sold away to an owner and place without any familiar faces nearby. She knew from the eviction of Giles, Paris, and Christopher Sheels from Philadelphia that this could happen at any time. In short, Ona had the same choices that she'd always had—which is to say, she didn't feel as though she had a choice. All she could do was work harder, work faster, and carry on.

But nothing was standing still, least of all Philadelphia in 1793. George Washington and the American colonists had sparked a series of uprisings around the globe. Revolution was in the air. A slave revolt in Haiti had led to the only slave rebellion in the Western Hemisphere where the slaves had won. In France, King Louis XVI and Marie Antoinette both went to the guillotine that year, and with their executions would go the French monarchy. In the sweaty summer streets of Philadelphia, abolitionists glared at slave owners in town for a congressional meeting. Slave owners glared back. No one paid special attention to a ship from the West Indies that had just docked five blocks away. They should have. The unwanted cargo that had stowed away on this ship was about to unleash the biggest panic the city had seen, and everyone would be affected.

ERICA ARMSTRONG DUNBAR and KATHLEEN VAN CLEVE

CHAPTER THIRTEEN
YELLOW FEVER

DURING THE SPRING OF 1793, ONA'S TIME WAS CONSUMED with all the social duties of the wife of the president and all the domestic duties that came with slavery. Whatever her wishes and dreams, Ona could not publicly pursue them. Her life was bent and shaped by the Washingtons' will.

Yet it was at this moment that the stowaways from the West Indies arrived: mosquitoes. Mosquitoes are always a pain. This time they were deadly. The mosquitoes didn't care what color a person's skin was; they just did what mosquitoes always do—bite. Soon men and women, black and white, old and young, rich and poor, began to get headaches. Then chills.

Then fevers. Eventually their organs failed. Death became the norm; yellow fever was sweeping through the city. Everyone suffered. No one figured out it was the mosquitoes that were spreading the disease.

Thousands of citizens fled. George and Martha ordered Ona and her fellow servants and slaves to pack up the household for a retreat to Mount Vernon. These were the days before modern medicine was considered a stable science. There were some educated guesses and some supernatural theories about the cause of the plague. Many people assumed that the sickness was caused by stale or smelly air; there were no sewage systems in the 1790s, and summers in Philadelphia were notoriously hot. This did not help the afflicted people, who were steaming from their fevers and vomiting from their infection.

It wasn't until the first frost swept over Philadelphia in November that the mosquitoes died off. Between four and five thousand white Philadelphians had died, as had four hundred black residents. Tobias Lear's wife, Polly, was one of the dead. Alexander Hamilton, the secretary of the treasury, and Richard Allen, the preacher, had both caught the disease but had managed to survive.

Ona was not in Philadelphia during the worst of the epidemic. She was with the rest of the household at Mount Vernon. If she had been there, she would have seen another example of how difficult it was to get white people and black people to live happily alongside one another.

When the disease was striking everyone in its path, Dr. Benjamin Rush, the most well-known of all the doctors in Philadelphia, came up with a hypothesis that people of African descent could not catch yellow fever. There was no basis for this theory, since indeed many black men and women in Philadelphia had been killed by the disease. Perhaps the relatively small number of black deaths compared to the total number of people who died made this fact unknown to Dr. Rush.

Whatever the reason, in September 1793, Dr. Rush reached out to leaders in the free black community, asking for their help as nurses and gravediggers. People were getting sick all over the place, and dead bodies were piling up and decomposing. The free black leaders Richard Allen and Absalom Jones heard Dr. Rush's plea, and they saw an opportunity to raise the status of free blacks in the city. If white people saw black men and women helping out during this horrible epidemic, these leaders reasoned, surely they would finally believe that this same community was worthy of freedom. Richard and Absalom also knew that people like Martha Washington had a stubborn belief in the negative stereotype of black people—that they were lazy, rebellious, and unreasonable. Richard and Absalom believed that helping out during the yellow fever epidemic was a chance to change their minds.

They rushed to help and brought with them many other black citizens eager to pitch in.

The entire effort was a catastrophe. Disease and death did not care what color skin a person had and struck blindly, and mercilessly, at everyone. Black people died of the disease at the same rate as white people. But just as black and white people were segregated in life, they were segregated in death. White bodies filled up white graves and black bodies filled up black graves at the same overwhelming pace.

What was even worse was that during the panic of the disease, white people began to accuse black people of robbing dying men and looting abandoned homes. An opportunity to reduce racial tension between black and white Philadelphians was lost. Instead the experience reminded free blacks, servants, and the enslaved that freedom, if and when it finally came, would not end years and years of racial violence, stereotypes, or wrongheaded hatred.

When Ona returned to Philadelphia with the Washingtons in late 1793, she would have walked among the wreckage of the city, noticing more than just grief in the air. She would have sensed that relations between blacks and whites had become even more hostile than they'd been when she had left. Soon she would hear firsthand how soul-crushing it was to be accused of such shameful behavior when the free black community had genuinely wanted to help. Richard Allen and Absalom Jones were more than aggrieved; they were furious. The same Matthew Carey who had published *Description of a Slave Ship* had printed a widely read pamphlet that accused black people of "plundering" white people's homes during the yellow fever epidemic. Richard and Absalom spent the next several months composing a response to Carey's destructive words. *To Those Who Keep Slaves and Approve the Practice* was printed in early 1794. In it, Richard campaigned not only for freedom for slaves but for a stop to racial discrimination.

> *If you love your children, if you love your country, if you love the God of love, clear your hands from slaves, burden not your children or your country with them.*

Even in Philadelphia, the place that would become the guiding star of the abolition movement, Richard's plea did not always work. For some white people, darker skin alone was reason to consider black people an inferior race. Even when black people offered up their lives to help whites, as they had during the yellow fever epidemic, they would still be rejected and scorned. This was a valuable lesson for the free black leaders like Richard Allen and Absalom Jones, but it was also a reminder to Ona herself that even if she somehow, some way, eventually claimed her freedom, it was not a ticket to an automatically easier life. Freedom did not erase racism. In fact, it could make racism worse.

Ona persisted, despite mounting despair. In December 1794 she met with a personal tragedy. Austin, now in his midthirties, was headed to see his wife, Charlotte, and their children at Mount Vernon. He often traveled alone during this journey from Philadelphia to Virginia and had always arrived at his destination safely. Not this time. Austin attempted to cross a river in Harford County, Maryland. It may have been a storm or a rushing current or something else altogether, but soon a letter arrived in Philadelphia stating that Austin was "with Great Difficulty . . . Dragged out of the water" and was "likely to Lose his Life."

He died shortly thereafter.

Ona was about twenty-one when she received even more devastating news in January 1795. Her mother, Betty, had died. She had gotten sick in her late fifties, and a lifetime of enslavement coupled with poor living conditions (particularly in the winter when cold air would come straight through the walls of the shabby slave cabins) meant that she was especially susceptible to illness. While George Washington may have been sympathetic, as a practical matter Betty's death saved him money. It cost money to shelter and feed and clothe elderly slaves who could no longer work. With her death, Betty had saved George this expense.

Ona had no reason to look at her loss practically. Betty was the only parent she had ever truly known. The death of Austin had been incredibly painful. And now her mother was gone. For Ona it must have been one of the most crushing blows of her short life.

Her trips to Mount Vernon would now be tinged with grief. Her life in Philadelphia was irrevocably changed, as the branches of her own family tree had been lopped off abruptly, leaving her basically alone. Philadelphia had much to commend itself over Mount Vernon, but as freed preacher Richard Allen stated, "Slavery is a bitter pill." Every life has ups and downs. Every life experiences sorrow. Disease can strike anyone, and death kills everyone. For slaves— for someone like Ona, living in the biggest city in the new country—the "ups" were never fully separated from fear. Every day, every second, Ona would have the worry that if she did something wrong, if she—perhaps—cried over the death of her mother instead of immediately serving Martha her tea—she might be sent away, back to Mount Vernon, or somewhere else.

Worse yet, human nature was allowed no outlet in the emotional life of the enslaved. There was no acceptable place for the range of human emotions. If you were angry, you had to swallow your rage. If you were afraid, you had to pretend as if you were calm. If your mother and brother had died a month apart, you had to go to work without tears, without a break, without comfort. Like a robot, a slave's life was programmed: Service to your owners. Sleep. Service. Sleep. Service. Repeat. The "ups" of a human life were limited to a trip to see a play (if you were lucky), an extra dress or pair of pants to wear (if you were lucky), a common-law wife or husband (if you were lucky). Ona was not lucky. But she was smart, and she was proud, and she was brave. It turned out that when things got even worse for her, these character traits would be enough.

MARTHA WAS GOING TO TURN SIXTY-FIVE IN 1796, AND HER life, as privileged as it was, had also hardened her. After all, she had lost all four of her children and her first husband. She had moved to the North when she considered herself completely a child of the South, and she had married a reserved man who had become the first president of the United States, which meant she would either have to travel all over the place to see him or stay home without him. She also had to carry the burden of the multitude of social events required of the president and his wife: dinner parties and other gatherings, entertaining important people from America and around the globe. On the surface this was not difficult for Martha; she was a masterful hostess, always gracious and witty. But in private, Martha was unpredictable.

Some days she would seem easygoing and patient. Other days she would snap at the slaves because of an accidentally overcooked meal or a candle not being instantly replaced. Ona had learned over the years to work alongside Martha even during her moodiest days. She had figured out how to tolerate Martha's outbursts by remaining calm at all times. It seemed that Ona had made some kind of peace with the future laid out in front of her.

But then the most unpredictable of emotions—love—changed Ona's life forever.

It was 1796. Martha Washington was consumed with planning a "birth night" ball to celebrate George's sixty-fourth birthday on February 22. This meant that Ona was also consumed with all the preparations, perhaps cleaning and hemming whatever dress Martha wanted to wear to the party.

Ona may have had a needle in hand, the dress on her knee, when the letter arrived. It was addressed to George Washington, although Martha's eyes would have widened when she recognized the writing. It was from her eldest granddaughter, Eliza Custis. Ona would have remembered her too. Eliza, about three years younger than Ona, the spoiled brat.

George and Martha read the letter immediately. It turned out that Eliza had urgent news to share, news that required the Washingtons' immediate attention. Eliza had fallen in love with a man named Thomas Law and wanted to be married as soon as possible. Wasn't it wonderful?

Ona could tell from the Washingtons' reactions that they did not think it was wonderful. And anyway, Ona would have her own private reaction. Eliza Custis had been a "mean girl" her whole life. She would be just the kind of person who would swoop into Martha's life right as she was planning a big party for her husband, so that everyone would have to think about Eliza.

Soon Ona would learn why, specifically, Eliza's news was not welcome. Eliza was nineteen. Thomas Law was thirty-eight. (Strike one.) Thomas Law was a British citizen who had lived in India for many years. (Strike two.) Thomas Law had several mixed-race children, even though he was not married. (Strike three.)

Thomas Law had moved to America when he'd learned about the creation of the new Federal City. Thomas, like many people called "speculators," believed that if he purchased some of the swampy land near the Potomac cheaply, it would rise in value once the Federal City was up and running. He bought hundreds of acres of land in northern Virginia. He was sure he would be rich. When he'd been buying up land, he'd met Eliza Custis. It is unknown whether he knew in advance that she was the step-granddaughter of the president.

Eliza knew that her marriage would need to be approved by the president. Perhaps this was why she asked her grandparents to wait to make a decision about this union until they heard from Thomas Law directly. He would, she told them, be writing them a letter very soon.

Out of all the strikes against Thomas Law, the most disturbing one was that he was a British citizen. If Eliza married him, he could force her to move to England, the country George had vanquished.

Then again, this was Eliza. Stubborn, rash, unkind, argumentative—Eliza had left a strong impression with many people. It was not a good one. Family members described Eliza as follows: "In her tastes and pastimes, she is more man than woman and regrets that she can't wear pants." Perhaps of all Eliza's unbecoming personality traits, her biggest flaw was that she was known to be unkind.

Ona, as usual, kept her mouth shut. When George received Thomas Law's letter shortly after receiving Eliza's, he discussed the potential marriage with

 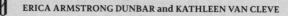ERICA ARMSTRONG DUNBAR and KATHLEEN VAN CLEVE

Martha. After much discussion, which Ona might have heard, they decided to approve the union.

George responded to Eliza's letter with the following:

> *If Mr. Law is the man of your choice, of which there can be no doubt, as he has merits to engage your affections, and you have declared that he has not only done so, but that you find, after a careful examination of your heart, you cannot be happy without him—that your alliance with him meets my approbation.*

Technically George had lied. Thomas Law's "alliance" with Eliza did not meet his "approbation." He did not like Thomas Law. He wished that Eliza would not marry him. But he and Martha had decided it was not worth the trouble to disagree with their tempestuous granddaughter.

For all intents and purposes, it seemed that the Washingtons had come to terms with Eliza's rash marriage plans. And while early America was very different from modern-day America, there was one impulse that remains strong to this day: gossip. The fact that Martha Washington's granddaughter was marrying someone twenty years older from another country—and the fact that she was doing it so quickly—was a source of great interest. Even John Adams, the vice president, wrote to his wife, Abigail, about Eliza's upcoming marriage, saying that Martha had told him the news in a "humorous style" even though Mr. Law "has two Children born in India: but of whom is not explained."

Over the years, Martha had taught herself how to behave publicly as if her entire life were perfect, even when that wasn't true. She was not happy about Eliza's marriage and was constantly trying to figure out a plan to "protect" her granddaughter from what she felt was a horrible decision. Yet in public she acted as if she could not be more pleased about the wedding, telling all who would listen about the event and the preparations. Only the people closest to her knew how upset she was.

Ona was one of those people. What she did not know—yet—was that she would be part of Martha's plan.

CHAPTER FIFTEEN

EXPECTATIONS

IN EARLY 1796 MASTER SWEEP AND BLACK RELIGIOUS leader Richard Allen visited one of his clients for his chimney-sweeping business: President George Washington. Chimney sweeping was a dirty, difficult business where the sweep had to squeeze down a brick chute and brush away accumulations of soot and dirt. But it paid well, and for a workaholic like Richard Allen, it was a job that gave him the income to pursue his advocacy for abolition and racial justice. Richard would have serviced the President's House himself, making sure that all the fireplaces in the mansion were usable. He would have known not to talk to George's slaves while he was working.

Not in public, anyway.

Meanwhile, on a beautiful estate in Virginia, Eliza Custis was about to marry her fiancé, Thomas Law. It was March 21, 1796, when Eliza and Thomas promised in front of their family and their pastor to live together for richer or poorer, in sickness and in health, as long as they both should live. (Or at least until their divorce, which was finalized in 1811.) Besides Eliza's wedding, the major news spreading through the Washington family—although not through the streets of the country—was that George had decided to retire from public service.

George Washington had been wrestling for many months with the question of whether to run for a third term. At the time of George's presidency, he could have continued to run for president as long as he liked, as it wasn't until 1951 that presidents were not allowed to serve more than two four-year terms. In fact, George's decision not to run for president after eight years is noteworthy because he essentially set the pattern for a peaceful transition of leadership for future presidencies. This remains one of the hallmarks of the United States—that is, since the country's inception, presidents who did not win subsequent elections have left the presidential office without attempting to stay in control.

This decision brought relief to both George and Martha. To their slaves, especially those who had lived with them in the North, the decision brought with it great anxiety. What was life at Mount Vernon going to hold for slaves like Ona, who had basically grown up in a northern city? How were the Washingtons going to treat her now that she would be part of the larger fold of enslaved black men and women, back in a place where the idea of any abolition act was absurd? Ona already knew how much George Washington disliked her sister Betty Davis. He had called her a "lazy, deceitful & impudent huzzy," and it would not have been surprising to anyone that upon the Washingtons' return to Mount Vernon, Betty Davis would be punished, perhaps severely. Could a similar fate await Ona? Was there any stability in her life that she could hold on to?

Actually, in Ona's mind, there was one source of stability.

Martha.

Ona had been a stellar example of a discreet, competent, respectful enslaved person. She had served Martha so well that she knew Martha needed her. Ona must have thought, *When I return to Mount Vernon, Martha will keep me by her side.*

There was no reason for her to think otherwise.

It turns out that Ona had grossly misjudged Martha. Martha did rely on Ona. In fact, she relied on her so much—and thought she was so spectacular—that Martha had come up with a way to manage her own anxiety about Eliza's wedding.

Eliza was a powder keg, everyone knew that. It was only a matter of time before she screwed up something as she arranged her new house, or yelled at her slaves, or fought with her new husband. Eliza needed calm. She needed a mood regulator. She needed Martha's own emotional temperature gauge.

In short, Eliza needed Ona.

Indeed, to Martha it was the perfect wedding gift. Though she would not wrap Ona up in pink wrapping paper with a *To Eliza, Congratulations! From Your Grandmother* tag, it was essentially the same thing. Martha refused to acknowledge the humanity of Ona, so it never occurred to Martha that her slave should not be treated as an object to be given away at her discretion. Although Ona was a human being, she was considered human property, and Martha had the right to give her to Eliza.

It is unknown how Ona found out she was to be a gift, or whether she was told by Martha directly. It is very likely that Martha never once considered how Ona would have felt, and it is probable that she did not

ERICA ARMSTRONG DUNBAR and KATHLEEN VAN CLEVE

spend a second thinking about how Ona would feel doomed if she even stepped foot in Eliza's house.

By April, Martha Washington made it known that she was giving her devoted slave, Ona Maria Judge, to her granddaughter, Eliza Custis Law, as a wedding gift.

Ona would not have had an opportunity to openly react to this sweeping, despicable news. She would not have been allowed to cry or complain or even say quietly, *I'd really prefer not to work for that brat, no offense.* She was expected to move to Virginia without complaint, to live with Eliza with the unpredictable temper, and Thomas, a man who had already proven himself to be willing to "befriend" women outside of marriage.

Ona had always done what was expected of her.

This time she would not.

CHAPTER SIXTEEN

THE PLANNING

DURING THE SPRING OF 1796, ONA JUDGE'S MIND WOULD HAVE been filled with dreams, nightmares, plans, and challenges. Every night, as she brushed Martha Washington's hair before bedtime, she would have to be careful not to tug too hard on the aging woman's scalp, no matter how furious she was that Martha had betrayed her so completely. Each morning, as she removed the stains from Martha's dresses and scraped the mud and dirt off Martha's shoes, she would have to stop herself from angrily ripping the dress and destroying the shoes, forcing herself to calm down and confront her future.

What Ona knew for sure was that she would never, ever be Eliza Parke Custis Law's slave. Not for one day, not for one hour, not for one second. Now she would have to figure out an exit plan.

In public Ona held her tongue. Just like Martha pretended to be happy about Eliza's wedding to Thomas Law, Ona pretended to be Martha's obedient slave. In reality Ona reached out for help.

The Underground Railroad did not yet exist. Harriet Tubman had not yet been born. The escape routes that the enslaved whispered about during the years leading up to the Civil War were still a fantasy. The rooms where slaves hid, the tunnels under the roads, the secret compartments in wagons—those were more than thirty years in the future. In 1796 slaves who planned their escape had fewer options. Many times they trusted the stories they had heard about escape routes—fleeing to the wilderness, hiding in an abandoned cabin, scrambling into a stone cavern. The goal was to get lost in a city or reach a free state, where they would be able to have a new identity, hiding from the nosy slave catchers who were poking around, looking for the easy reward of turning in a fugitive slave.

Ona had the added challenge of wanting to escape from the most important person in the country. More challenges: She was in a city where everyone knew who she was. She did not know how to read or write. Most of all, she was terrified.

But her anger helped. Whenever she thought about it, she could still not believe that Martha was going to give her as a gift—like a piece of china!—to a woman who everyone knew was impossible. Every time Ona thought about this, it reinforced her decision to leave. She had to make a plan and she had to carry it out.

It was clear to Ona and most of the other slaves in Philadelphia that the life of a fugitive slave was dangerous. Despite the gradual abolition laws in some of the northern states, several hurdles stood in the way of the men and women who escaped. The most obvious hurdle was weather. Northeastern winters were ice cold, literally freezing one of the main routes of escape—the rivers and creeks. It was hard enough to get a warm coat or shoes when you were enslaved, particularly if you were from one of the southern states. To be on the run, in a threadbare coat, was asking for hypothermia, or death. Escaping during the spring and summer was not much easier. Fugitives were just as susceptible to heat and humidity as they were to brutal cold; they could die from dehydration, starvation, or heatstroke.

Ona's escape deadline would be determined by the date when she would be expected to join Eliza's new team of house slaves near the Federal City, where the newlyweds had purchased a home. Presumably, Martha thought Ona should move in with Eliza and Thomas when the rest of the Washington household packed up to travel to Mount Vernon for the summer.

Ona also faced a familiar and frustrating obstacle—her gender. Ninety percent of fugitive slaves, from Pennsylvania down to Virginia, were male. The reason was pretty simple: children.

Marriages between slaves were not recognized by the law. But as always, people fell in love and wanted to remain with their partners and begin families of their own. Throughout the plantation-filled South, many enslaved women fell in love and had children. Many enslaved women were not in love but still had children. What was true for just about all of them was that they were responsible for their children. Even if fathers wanted to be involved in their children's lives, they were sometimes working in fields far away from their wives. If and when an enslaved father decided to escape, he would more than likely go it alone.

The age range of most fugitives was between sixteen and thirty-five. Not coincidentally, this was also the exact age span when enslaved women tended to be pregnant, feeding, or caring for a child. Even if a woman with a child had the opportunity to escape, it was often an impossible decision for her to make. If she left her child behind, the child could be whipped. If she took her child with her, she would most likely get caught. An infant's cries of hunger would shatter the necessary silence of a fugitive's flight. A small child would be unable to keep up with adults literally running for their lives. For many of the enslaved women, there was simply no choice. They would remain slaves because their priority was to care for their children, no matter the cost to themselves.

Ona had managed to reach the age of twenty-three without having children. If she escaped, she would likely never see her sisters and brother at Mount Vernon again.

This was painful, but it was not the same agony as having to leave one's child behind, or else risk that child's safety by taking him or her along on the run.

Ona's youth and her childlessness would aid in her escape. What would stop her in her tracks was the overwhelming fear of what could happen if she were caught, captured, and returned to the Washingtons. She was right to be afraid.

George Washington was extremely vigilant about any and all escape attempts from Mount Vernon, even while he was living in Philadelphia. He would also punish or sell difficult slaves when he thought it was appropriate, even though he maintained that he did not like to rip apart the families of the enslaved. During the early 1790s, George sold at least two slaves

ERICA ARMSTRONG DUNBAR and KATHLEEN VAN CLEVE

after he determined that they could not be controlled. He wrote his Mount Vernon estate manager, Anthony Whiting, that he would take action if a third slave named Ben refused to behave:

> If a stop is not put to his rogueries, and other villanies by fair means and shortly; that I will ship him off (as I did Waggoner Jack) for the West Indies, where he will have no opportunity of playing such pranks as he is at present engaged in.

Waggoner Jack had been sold for a quantity of wine.

Physical harm was the other weapon George Washington and other slave owners used as a way to control their enslaved population. Ona's sister-in-law, Charlotte, Austin's widow, was the victim of such physical abuse.

In January 1793, almost two years before Austin's death, Charlotte had defied Anthony Whiting, and he wrote George that he "gave . . . a very good Whipping" and that he was "determined to lower her Spirit or skin her Back." George responded to Whiting, agreeing with his handling of Charlotte and stating, "And if she, or any other—of the Servants, will not do their duty by fair means—or are impertinent, correction (as the only alternative) must be administered."

George believed that he was a fair slave owner. The scars on his slaves' backs would probably argue otherwise.

Now was the time when Ona could take advantage of living in a city with such a thriving population of freed black men and women. They would help her. Luck was on Ona's side in this way: the one man who could and did help runaways regularly visited her house.

The preacher, cobbler, and chimney sweep Richard Allen could offer assistance.

CHAPTER SEVENTEEN

THE *NANCY*

BASED ON A RECEIPT FOR HIS CHIMNEY SWEEPING services, Richard Allen was in the President's House in March 1796. Ona would have made contact with him during one of his visits—maybe signaling to him that she wanted to talk. Perhaps they moved behind a staircase, or maybe she dusted a fireplace mantel as he knelt down to the iron grate holding the ashes. It would have taken just a few minutes for Ona to ask him for help; Richard Allen would have kept his answer short, probably just nodding. Ona would have moved quickly away from the fireplace. She was scared, of course. But she was hopeful.

On May 10, 1796, it is likely that Ona left the

President's House to complete a few errands, including the purchase of a new pair of shoes. She would have to walk only five blocks, from Market Street to Spruce Street, to find the shoemaker she most wanted to visit: Richard Allen.

We can't know for certain whether Richard Allen and Ona talked about an escape, because there's no proof of the conversation. There were no voice recorders back then. But it would be really surprising if they didn't. Richard Allen was an ex-slave himself; he would understand what it would mean to help a scared but brave enslaved woman. He would understand too that if Ona were to flee, it would be a bigger deal than the escape of other runaways. It was not often that anyone, let alone an enslaved woman, took on the famed military hero and first president of the United States, George Washington.

May 10 was a Tuesday. If Ona had figured out a plan with Richard Allen to escape, she would have learned that she needed to wait for an appropriate ship with an obliging ship captain in order to successfully flee Philadelphia. Perhaps there was a way for Richard Allen to get messages to Ona, telling her on what day she needed to be ready? Or perhaps there was a network of free black men and women who managed to pass bits of important information to Ona without

ERICA ARMSTRONG DUNBAR and KATHLEEN VAN CLEVE

anyone else knowing? No matter what, Ona had to calm her nerves and raise no suspicions as she packed for the upcoming summer trip to Mount Vernon, as if she were really going to take that journey. Ona already knew that she was not going anywhere near Virginia, as she later recalled, "I knew that if I went back to Virginia, I never should get my liberty."

Although the president and his wife possessed more slaves and servants than did most slave owners in northern residences, Ona was the person who needed to be available to them around the clock. But working for Martha for so long had its advantages. Ona knew the routine of the household. There was one part of each day when Ona did not have to be present: dinner.

Hercules and his kitchen staff were in charge of most things related to food. When the food was on the table, one of the waiters, not Ona, would bring seconds, or refill wineglasses, or pick up the dirty plates. This was Ona's window of opportunity.

Did Ona tell Hercules about her plans? We don't know. But if she did, he may have deliberately served the president's favorite food, salted fish. The best-case scenario for Ona would be that George and Martha would linger over their meal, perhaps asking for seconds. This would give Ona a much-needed head start.

On Saturday, May 21, 1796, eleven days after she

brought back new shoes, the Washingtons sat down in their first-floor dining room. Their dinner was served. Ona may have cast her eyes around, taking in every last detail of the President's House. Maybe she met eyes with Hercules in the kitchen. Or maybe she just turned and walked out.

As soon as she was outside, Ona would have followed the orders she'd received from the free black friends who were brave enough to help her. Walk east five blocks, straight to the Philadelphia shipyard. Wear the coarse, modest clothes of free black women, not the brighter gowns allowed for the slave of the president. Keep your eyes straight ahead and pull your bag close to your body. Look for a ship with a single sail; it will be the one loading a bunch of saddles and potatoes.

The ship's name was the *Nancy* (though Ona would not have been able to read it), and the captain's name was John Bowles. Ona was given one rule: never say his name aloud.

John Bowles was not publicly known as someone who fought against slavery. His name did not appear on the list of prominent New England abolitionists, nor was he mentioned when people talked about the anti-slavery activists fighting against southern and northern slave owners. He ran his shipping business with a partner, Thomas Leigh, and had been traveling up and down the East Coast, transporting various goods, for years.

In early May 1796 the Portsmouth Customs House in New Hampshire cleared the *Nancy*'s voyage to Philadelphia. Most likely, Bowles sailed directly there, a trip that would have taken four to five days. The *Philadelphia Gazette* announced Bowles's arrival in the city on May 10, the very same day that Ona bought new shoes. For almost two weeks Bowles advertised his goods for sale and offered room on his ship to anyone who wanted to travel to New Hampshire. Eventually Bowles loaded molasses, coffee, potatoes, boots, bridles, saddles, and candles onto his ship.

He also allowed Ona Judge to walk on board.

It is possible that Ona's elegant attitude led Bowles to believe she was a free woman instead of a slave. More likely is that he had been expecting her. It was strange for a young woman at that time, white or black, to travel without a chaperone. If he had believed that she was a free woman traveling, he would probably have stopped and questioned her. But he didn't. Whether he'd been contacted in advance by someone working on her behalf, or whether he just recognized a desperate spirit, Captain Bowles turned a blind eye to Ona.

Pounding heart, terrified spirit, Ona counted the seconds until she could feel the ship lurch on the water, finally untied from the dock. She probably spent her time on the ship reviewing the words of her allies.

Someone will meet you when the ship docks.

Do not ever say John Bowles's name.

We can't tell you where you're going, for your sake; if you do get caught, you can't get anyone in trouble.

Keep your mouth shut and your head down, and pray.

It's hard to even imagine when she let herself take her first deep breath of freedom. Perhaps it was up on the deck, as the Delaware River merged into the Atlantic Ocean. The *Nancy* was a small ship, eclipsed by the larger boats pushing their wares up and down the coastline. Some of those ships contained Africans, chained together just as described in Matthew Carey's broadside. Other ships carried sugar and tobacco from the Americas over to Europe. As the ships crisscrossed, the *Nancy* sailed northward. Ona, the American-born slave to the president, had leaped boldly into the next phase of her life.

It wasn't easy. The crashing waves of the Atlantic hurled saddles and candles from one side of the storage hold to another. The smell of molasses and coffee was thick. The combination of odors and the rocking sea were overpowering. The *Nancy* was not a luxury vessel; it was an older, uninspected ship with torn sails and weathered wood, hoping to make it to the next

ERICA ARMSTRONG DUNBAR and KATHLEEN VAN CLEVE

port without incident. Space was minimal, and travelers slept wherever there was room. When the ship tilted or water crashed over the sides, Ona must have felt sick.

But not as sick as when she tried to prepare herself for the new set of monsters that would be waiting for her after the Washingtons discovered that she had escaped.

Slave catchers.

Ona would have to stay on her guard.

CHAPTER EIGHTEEN

NEW HAMPSHIRE: LIVE FREE OR DIE!

ON MAY 23, 1796, THE *PHILADELPHIA GAZETTE* PUBLISHED an advertisement. The next day, a second Philadelphia newspaper, *Claypoole's American Daily Advertiser*, published the same ad.

TEN DOLLARS REWARD, the headline exclaimed, and it was followed by a description of Ona Judge.

> Absconded from the household of the President of the United States, on Saturday afternoon, Oney Judge, a light Mulatto girl, much freckled, with very black eyes, and bushy black hair—she is of middle stature, but slender and delicately made, about 20

years of age. She has many changes of very good clothes of all sorts, but they are not suffciently recollected to describe.

As there was no suspicion of her going off, and it happened without the least provocation, it is not easy to conjecture whither she is gone—or fully, what her design is; but as she may attempt to escape by water, all masters of vessels and others are cautioned against receiving her on board, altho' she may, and probably will endeavor to pass for a free woman, and it is said has, wherewithal to pay her passage.

Ten dollars will be paid to any person, (white or black) who will bring her home, if taken in the city, or on board any vessel in the harbor; and a further reasonable sum if apprehended and brought home, from a greater distance, and in proportion to the distance.

May 24 FRED. KITT, Steward.

Descriptions of runaway slaves ran in newspapers all the time. But this advertisement was shocking because it announced that an enslaved woman had "absconded"—from the *president of the United States*.

No one knows exactly when Martha or George realized that Ona was missing. It probably was the night she left or the next morning. Had Martha been waiting for Ona to brush her hair? Had George been expecting Ona to carry Martha's bag down the stairs?

"Oney?" We can hear them call. "Oney? Where are you?"

No answer.

Martha may not have worried until a few minutes turned into ten. Twenty.

Could she? Would she? *How dare she?*

Forget about the impoliteness of now not having a "gift" for Eliza. Now Martha felt as if Ona Judge had humiliated her in public. George must have had to listen to Martha's cries about Ona's ingratitude.

"The girl . . . was brought up & treated more like a child than a servant," he later wrote.

By the time they calmed down and devised a plan, Ona had a big head start. By now she would have learned that she was on her way to a state way up in the North, Tobias Lear's home state, New Hampshire. Ona may have remembered this, just as she may have remembered that she had met a member of probably the most respected family in New Hampshire—Senator John Langdon. Ona would certainly have remembered

Senator Langdon's daughter, Elizabeth, who was the same age as Nelly, Martha's granddaughter, and whom Ona might have watched when the Langdon family had visited Philadelphia.

Like the rest of the northern states, New Hampshire was moving fitfully toward abolition. On the plus side, the state's Bill of Rights specified that every citizen of New Hampshire was promised equality and liberty. On the minus side, slavery had been legal since the colony had first been established in 1641. In the 1780s, when Ona had first moved north, New Hampshire had finally begun to make progress toward outlawing slavery. But it wasn't until 1857 that the state outlawed slavery altogether.

Luckily for Ona, she was arriving in Portsmouth, New Hampshire—a town that would declare itself free from slavery in 1805, fifty-two years earlier than the state itself.

When the *Nancy* tied up against the wooden dock, Ona would have probably left the ship as quickly as she could, her eyes scanning the strangers to see if anyone sparked any kind of recognition. Her first priority was to find a place to live, no easy task for a single black woman with very little money. But the network of free black allies had worked. People were expecting her. Someone—we don't know who—met her at the dock.

She was soon directed to her temporary home, with a free black family.

Philadelphia and Portsmouth had two things in common: they both had prominent shipyards, and they were both ahead of the curve with respect to slavery. Other than that, they were vastly different. Portsmouth was tiny, with only about five thousand residents, and there were fewer black people in the entire city of Portsmouth than there were slaves living at Mount Vernon! The only benefit to this was that Ona would soon grow to know the majority of the black community.

But she didn't have time yet to meet people. Her priority was to get a job. She had been sewing all her life and had designed and stitched together some of Martha's beautiful gowns. In today's world she might have been a fashion designer. Without letters of recommendation vouching for her actual expertise, Ona had to tell potential employers that she was fit for all kinds of domestic work.

Ona was smart, quick-witted, and nimble. But she was not prepared for all kinds of work. She had to learn fast. Besides doing laundry and housecleaning, Ona would have to pick up cooking skills. Perhaps in a household other than the Washingtons', Ona would have learned how to cook. With Hercules around—an

ERICA ARMSTRONG DUNBAR and KATHLEEN VAN CLEVE

early American celebrity chef—she had stayed away from the kitchen. So cooking was something she would have to learn on the fly; all households needed someone who knew how to prepare the basic meals for a family. Further, in Portsmouth a domestic servant was expected to do *all* domestic work: carry heavy cauldrons of water, sew dresses, *and* make dinner.

Once again it appears that Ona's black allies in Portsmouth stepped in. They likely spent time teaching her what she would have to do. Then they got her a job. Two facts stand out. One: the majority of black women in New England at the time did not live beyond the age of forty. And two: the majority of black women in New England were employed as domestic workers. There was a connection between the two; the domestic work was nonstop and grueling.

But Ona *got paid*. From the outside, if you didn't know her past, you would think she was just a free black woman, working hard to get a small (but appreciated and deserved) salary. It would be fair to assume that she was overworked and underpaid, which she certainly was. But it would also be fair to assume that all the work and all the pay was worth it to Ona because of the basic fact that she was living the way she—not Martha, not George—chose to live.

She was still scared. She knew that the Washingtons

would soon be on her trail. So Ona, as she always did, kept quiet and listened. Portsmouth was not perfect and neither was New Hampshire, but people like John Bowles and her new free black friends had convinced her that her relocation to Portsmouth was strategic and potentially rewarding. She never stopped looking over her shoulder for slave catchers, but for the first time since she had heard that she would be given away as a wedding gift, she let herself take a deep breath, and hope.

ERICA ARMSTRONG DUNBAR and KATHLEEN VAN CLEVE

CHAPTER NINETEEN

ELIZABETH LANGDON

PORTSMOUTH WAS A QUAINT AND INTIMATE NEW ENGLAND shipping town with small streets and a passionate, hardworking citizenry. It was a place where Ona could hide, and provided she kept a low profile, she could buy whatever food she liked at the market with her earnings. She could repay the generosity of her hosts by bringing home turnips or a fish called striped bass. She could even begin to sew again, perhaps making some dresses for her hosts and then, eventually, buying enough material and ribbons and buttons so that she could create elaborate gowns like the ones she used to make for Martha Washington. Freedom had been her first objective. Lifting herself up from a crippling, life-sapping poverty would be her second.

Of course, Ona always knew she was not legally free. She would never be unless Martha Washington would agree to free her slaves, and Ona knew better than anyone else that Martha would never, ever do that. Ona was probably haunted by nightmares about the treatment of her siblings and nieces left behind at Mount Vernon. She probably could imagine the strong arms and greedy eyes of the violent slave catchers searching for her, the slave who'd had the audacity to flee the president of the United States. The good news was that Ona was establishing a solid reputation among her new townspeople. The bad news was that it turned out that the Langdons, who could have lived anywhere in New Hampshire, lived in Portsmouth too.

Senator John Langdon, the head of this prominent family, had been born in 1741, nine years after George Washington, and unlike many wealthy and sophisticated men of his social class, he had decided not to go to college. Like many other men in Portsmouth, John chose to work in the very lucrative shipping trade, where he could sell goods up and down the East Coast. Eventually he purchased his own fleet of vessels. In fact, if the British hadn't gotten in his way on the trade routes in the Atlantic Ocean, John Langdon might

ERICA ARMSTRONG DUNBAR and KATHLEEN VAN CLEVE

never have become one of the leaders on the American side of the Revolutionary War.

But the British did get in the way. They started to charge American ships for passage on the Atlantic, and this made John irate because he was losing money. When he had a chance to ally himself with the Americans against the British, he jumped at it.

There was exactly one military post in New Hampshire. It was called Fort William and Mary, and it was controlled by the British. It was full of gunpowder, cannons, and ammunition. In 1774 John led a group of other men from Portsmouth in a military operation where they took over the fort, seizing all the gunpowder and ammunition. He became a hero for this daring—some would say reckless—act. Soon John was also a political leader, attending many of the big political events of the era.

In 1776 he was part of the Second Continental Congress. This was the time when the United States officially declared war on England, and the only reason he did not sign the Declaration of Independence was because he left the Continental Congress early to fight with the New Hampshire militia. In 1787 John was in Philadelphia at the Constitutional Convention, signing the new US Constitution. After the war was over, he became the first president of the United States Senate.

In 1796, when Ona arrived in Portsmouth, John was still serving as a US senator.

John had met and worked with George Washington on many occasions. In November 1789 George wrote in his diary about visiting John in New Hampshire: "Portsmouth, it is said, contains about 5,000 inhabitants. There are some good houses, (among which Col. Langdon's may be esteemed the first)."

When the Langdons went to Philadelphia, it made all the adults pleased when they watched their descendants play together. Elizabeth Langdon and Nelly Washington represented a new kind of American royalty, one the daughter of a senator, the other the granddaughter of the president of the United States. They grew up privileged, aware that because of who their father and grandfather were, a spotlight followed them around.

Ona could remember the times in Philadelphia when Moll had needed help and Ona had had to join in with the caregiving of Nelly, perhaps serving Elizabeth and Nelly tea or accompanying them to a cultural event in Philadelphia, even though Ona was only a few years older than the girls. More than anyone else in Portsmouth, it was Elizabeth Langdon, now eighteen, who scared Ona the most. She probably figured out where the Langdons lived and tried to stay away.

ERICA ARMSTRONG DUNBAR and KATHLEEN VAN CLEVE

Ona learned her new city. She found the markets and the churches. She met with other free blacks, some of whom knew who she was and some of whom just accepted her as a free woman doing her best to get by, just like they all were. Most of her time was spent working and learning the ropes of her new job. She started to walk taller, more proudly, as if she had never been enslaved. It was a performance that all fugitive slaves had to perfect; you couldn't act like you were scared of being caught when you were in public. But soon Ona began to feel more and more natural as she walked down Gardner Street and over to Walton Alley to get ingredients to make dinner.

It felt good to be free—or at least to live freely. It felt good to keep her head up, not down. It felt good to be recognized by new friends.

She may have been thinking about this on the day when she walked down a street and found her eyes landing on the person coming toward her from the other direction.

Elizabeth Langdon.

Ona froze. Elizabeth Langdon may have smiled. Ona summoned all her personal strength and stopped herself from running away as fast as she could. Portsmouth was too small—there was no safe space for her to hide. Even more, she instantly realized that running would have been the worst possible reaction. She would cause a scene, drawing attention to herself. It was a surefire way to be caught.

She took a deep breath and made a decision, one that probably felt staggeringly significant. For her entire life, she had learned how to hide her feelings—erasing anger from her face while it boiled in her heart, holding back tears while they flooded the wells of her eyes. But at this second, Ona knew she had to rely on her skill as an expert of being invisible. Lowering her head, she began to walk with purpose, avoiding Elizabeth's eyes and stepping past her without any kind of acknowledgment.

Elizabeth Langdon would have been confused. As the daughter of the most prominent man in town, she would have learned to ignore the people who stared at her because of her family. But this was different. The face of the young black woman was so familiar—Elizabeth was certain she had seen her before. But where?

Meanwhile, Ona continued to walk as her mind filled with images of ruin, each more awful than the last. Once again she may have remembered the looks on those women from long ago—Lucy and Esther—the enslaved women who had fled to the British during the war but who had returned, skeletons of their former selves. Ona had to leave Portsmouth. But where could she go? Where would she hide? If she returned to her hosts' home, the people who had put their own lives on the line in order to give her shelter, they could be arrested under the Fugitive Slave Act for hiding a fugitive. Yet what else could she do? She had to tell her hosts. Maybe they could come up with a plan. She started to walk more quickly, thoughts racing through her mind.

Maybe Elizabeth *hadn't* recognized her?

Maybe Elizabeth wouldn't turn her in if she had?

Meanwhile, Elizabeth Langdon had a million of her own thoughts racing through her mind. She had figured it out. The woman she had seen was indeed the slave who used to serve Martha Washington in Philadelphia when Elizabeth would visit with her family. But what on earth was Ona doing in Portsmouth, and where was Mrs. Washington? Surely Elizabeth would have heard if the president and his family were in New Hampshire. For a moment she second-guessed herself. The only other reason for Ona to be in Portsmouth was so unimaginable that it was absurd.

Right?

Elizabeth knew what she had to do. She had to tell her father.

Ona, back at her hosts' home, told them what had happened. She had probably calmed down. She couldn't stay hidden forever. If it hadn't been Elizabeth Langdon, it could just as easily have been Tobias Lear, visiting his family in Portsmouth. Ona was living as a free woman. This, then, was the cost. She would wait and see what happened.

Elizabeth told her father that she had seen Ona on the street in Portsmouth. Senator John Langdon must have been shocked that Ona was in his state, but he would not have been shocked that she had escaped. All of George's friends and acquaintances—indeed, people who didn't know George Washington personally at all—had read that one of his slaves, a girl, had walked out of his home one evening and run away. John just hadn't expected her to land here, in his own hometown.

When Elizabeth heard about Ona's escape, she may have reacted like many other wealthy slave owners, asking, *Why would Ona escape at all?*

For people like the Langdons, it was difficult to accept that black people would even have the initiative and intelligence to risk escape. The Langdon family did not own any slaves in 1796, but they had owned them in the past, and like the Washingtons, the Langdons had been paternalistic owners who had considered themselves to be compassionate and generous. They thought they were different from the "cruel" slave owners—the people who used the whip as a torture device, as opposed to using it only to make sure their slaves did their jobs. The Langdons had given their slaves more opportunities to do things on their own, more than the bare minimum of clothes and food. In short, in their minds, they had been noble, caring and providing for people whom they believed to be incapable of caring for themselves. In truth, they were not noble or caring: they had participated in a system that dehumanized other humans. It was an excuse to continue buying and selling other humans.

It's possible that Senator Langdon and his daughter even spoke of Ona's ingratitude. They knew that the Washingtons had offered pocket money to their slaves and had allowed them to attend the theater. They knew that George, like the Langdons, had tried to keep slave families together. In their minds, George and Martha were some of the *good* owners, wise and well-mannered in the way of the "good" southern families. Why would any slave run away, especially Ona, who had been Martha's favorite?

Perhaps if Elizabeth Langdon had known of the plan for Ona to be given away to horrible Eliza Custis Law, she might have understood why Ona had felt she had to leave. But maybe not. Eliza was a terrible person, but there were a lot of terrible people. Why would that be enough for any slave to risk so much?

It would have been impossible for Elizabeth Langdon or her father to understand what it was like to live as a slave. It was equally incomprehensible to people like them why Ona would want to free herself. Further, John Langdon was a senator of the United States of America, and he was obligated to follow the law. Ona Judge was a fugitive. The Washingtons owned her. To the Langdons, Ona was as much the property of the Washingtons as their dining room table or their horses were. The president needed to be told immediately.

John Langdon sat down to write a letter to his friend, the president. It took several days for the letter to reach Philadelphia. The Washingtons had spent the summer at Mount Vernon and had only just returned to Philadelphia themselves. The letter was waiting for them. On August 21, 1796, George opened it.

He now knew exactly where to find Ona Judge.

CHAPTER TWENTY

THE LAWBREAKER

GEORGE HAD A LOT GOING ON WHEN HE RETURNED FROM Mount Vernon in August 1796—a lot going on besides his effort to capture his runaway slave, Ona Judge.

Most important, he had to tell the citizens of the United States that he had decided to retire. He had originally written a "farewell address" with the help of James Madison in 1792, when he'd thought he would retire after one term. Now, after two terms, he asked his friend Alexander Hamilton to help him compose the news. On September 19, 1796, the Philadelphia newspaper *Claypoole's American Daily Advertiser* printed George Washington's official announcement.

Attention turned to politics and who was going to

take George's place as president. George and Martha were free to plan for their return to Mount Vernon.

Ona had complicated this return. Even without the Internet, if George Washington got caught up in a public battle to capture a young female slave, everyone would hear about it. The country's battle over slavery was getting worse, not better. In his mind, he had spent his entire life in public service and did not want to ruin that reputation by getting in the middle of the slavery question, which had thwarted the country from its very beginning.

At the same time, George was *really* mad. Martha was out of her mind. This was the second time in one year that a young woman had upended their lives—first their granddaughter Eliza Custis Law, and now Ona. But Eliza was always unpredictable. Moreover, she had only gotten married. Ona had humiliated them. Runaways reminded Americans that slaves were people, not simply property, even if they worked for the president and were able to wear nicer clothes. Ona's very escape proved that the idea of a "benevolent slave owner" was a lie. Enslavement was never preferable over freedom, even if you got to wear pretty gowns.

Even with the law on his side, if George pursued Ona, he would create a huge public relations problem. Attitudes in the United States had continued to change during the seven years since he'd become president. The changes weren't even all related to slavery. In 1787, for example, after the Constitution had been approved, those people who favored a strong central government had won. This group of people had become known as the Federalists. George Washington was never a formal member of this party, but certainly he had supported a stronger central government, along with Alexander Hamilton, John Adams, and New Hampshire senator John Langdon.

By George's second term, a group of people who called themselves anti-federalists argued that it had been wrong to make a strong federal government and that they wanted to put more power in the control of the individual states. Thomas Jefferson and James Madison were a part of this group. Many other major political leaders were changing their minds, including John Langdon.

At the same time, slavery was still a crucial issue that had not been figured out. Generally speaking, the North wanted slavery to be abolished and the South did not. Ona's escape had placed George in a difficult position. Even though he felt that he had been bitterly, badly treated by a freckle-faced, bushy-haired young black woman, if he pursued Ona, he would risk a public battle. On the other hand, if he didn't try to capture her, she would . . . "win."

George's anger was a matter of pride.

Because of Ona, the Washingtons had already clamped down on the number of slaves returning to Philadelphia after the summer in Mount Vernon. Only two slaves were permitted to accompany George and Martha: Moll, the now almost-fifty-seven-year-old babysitter, and Joe Richardson, a new postilion to replace Paris and Giles. Otherwise, the Washingtons used northern white servants. This put Martha on edge. None of the replacements seemed to be as efficient as her previous staff, especially Ona. None of them could anticipate her moods or calm her down when she was upset. Martha seethed that Ona had left her; she took it personally. George, the most powerful man in America, was a devoted husband.

It was pretty simple. Martha wanted Ona back. George needed to get her back.

Still, he took his time to figure out a plan. His first decision was that Ona's escape was not only his problem; it was also the *government's* problem. She had run away when he was president. Therefore, he reasoned, he was allowed to involve various government officials in her capture. He approached the secretary of the treasury, Oliver Wolcott Jr., about his situation.

Oliver agreed to help. George sat down the next day to write to Oliver about Ona and getting her back to Virginia.

The more he wrote, the angrier he became. In *his* mind, they had treated Ona like their own child! She had lived with him in *three* president's homes, not just one! Ona knew everything about his and Martha's personal life—they had even shared a bedroom door! With each word he wrote, his fingers moved faster across the page, his anger matching his intensity.

George told Oliver about his suspicion that the real reason Ona had left his household was because she had fallen in love with someone, a Frenchman, to be specific, who had then abandoned her. None of this was true. The problem was that in George's quest to understand Ona's escape, he had fallen back on a wrongheaded assessment of women, rather than accepting the immorality of slavery. In his opinion women were not as smart as men, and black women were even less smart. They were emotional wrecks. Ona was just not clever or capable enough to have done all this herself. The Frenchman had lured her away and now—probably—Ona was alone on the streets, begging.

What choice did he have, George wrote, but to track her down? Ona was in danger!

He then suggested to Oliver how he thought the

apprehension of Ona Judge should be completed. First Oliver should contact the customs officer in Portsmouth, a man named Joseph Whipple. Joseph would act as George's spy, finding out where Ona was and what she was doing. Then, George instructed, Joseph should find her and "put her on board a vessel bound immediately to this place, or to Alexandria which I should like better."

Remember the phrase called "due process" in the Constitution? And remember the Fugitive Slave Act that George Washington himself had signed into law? Since Ona was a fugitive, the law said that if she was found, the slave owner must bring the fugitive in front of a judge in the state to which she had escaped (New Hampshire), and the slave owner must provide proof of his ownership before he could take the slave with him out of the state. Ona did not have many rights, but she did have at least this one: if George wanted her back, she was supposed to receive "due process" and be able to go in front of a New Hampshire judge.

George had no intention of bringing Ona in front of any judge. He himself had no intention of going in front of any judge.

George Washington was, in other words, breaking *his own law.* And he was asking Oliver Wolcott and Joseph Whipple to break the law too.

In his letter George assured Oliver that his suggestions would prove "the safest & least expensive" and, not coincidentally, he added that Joseph would be compensated for any and all costs associated with the capture and return of his fugitive slave, along with earning the abundant appreciation of George Washington himself. Who wouldn't want to be in the good graces of the president, the most respected man in America, even if it meant breaking the law?

It turned out that Joseph Whipple did not.

CHAPTER TWENTY-ONE

THE NEGOTIATOR

JOSEPH WHIPPLE WAS A LITTLE YOUNGER THAN THE president and had lived his entire life in New Hampshire. His family was prominent. Joseph's brother, General William Whipple Jr., had been a soldier in the Revolutionary War, an associate justice of the New Hampshire Superior Court, and a signer of the Declaration of Independence. The Whipples had also owned slaves for much of the eighteenth century, but by the 1780s they had begun to free their slaves, starting with those enslaved men who'd fought in the Revolution.

In fact, it was their slave, the famed Prince Whipple, who had served in the American Army and been rewarded for his service with freedom. Previously owned by William Whipple, Prince Whipple later became well known because everyone thought he was the black soldier in the famous painting of George Washington crossing the Delaware. He was not that soldier, but by the time people found this out, it didn't matter. His was the name that people remembered.

Joseph Whipple was friends with Senator John Langdon. It was John's recommendation to George Washington that had led to Joseph's appointment as Portsmouth's customs collector. Joseph Whipple was another example of the changing mind-sets of people in the late 1700s. With his family freeing their slaves, and with him rethinking his own Federalist feelings, he was disturbed when he received the request for help from the president. George's apparent bitterness about Ona's behavior was obvious.

> *The ingratitude of the girl, who was brought up & treated more like a child than a servant (& Mrs. Washington's desire to recover her) ought not to escape with impunity if it can be avoided.*

"Ought not to escape with impunity" was a fancy way of saying that Ona's escape was such an insult to the Washingtons that it was important she be punished for even having the desire to be free.

Then again, this was a request from the president. When Oliver Wolcott told Joseph Whipple in Portsmouth of the president's request, Joseph agreed to investigate Ona.

Joseph spent the next several weeks searching for Ona. He probably started by going to the docks, asking ship captains and merchant friends if they had seen a young black woman with freckles and bushy hair. He would not have mentioned that she was a runaway, or that she had fled the president. No one was able to help.

Joseph came up with a new plan, a more deceptive one. A woman like Ona would probably need a good job, and what would be better than a job with a well-known member of Portsmouth's community like him? He told acquaintances that his household was in need of a good servant who would help his wife, Hannah, with traditional housework. Joseph probably made sure to ask free blacks—those who served as maids and waiters to his friends—if they knew anyone who was in the market for a job.

The plan worked. Ona immediately applied for employment with the Whipples. Friends would have told her about Joseph and his relatively famous family, which would have made her realize that this was

ERICA ARMSTRONG DUNBAR and KATHLEEN VAN CLEVE

exactly the kind of work she had performed for the Washingtons. Further, the job would seem to have the potential to become a permanent one, especially if Ona worked as hard as she always did. The temporary jobs available to Ona for the previous few months had been constantly changing, and like anyone, she wanted solid and stable employment. Finally, Ona would have been pleased to learn that the Whipples did not own slaves. The position probably sounded too good to be true.

And it was.

Soon Ona was on her way to meet Joseph for an interview. Joseph would have been prepared. He might have reviewed the advertisement the Washingtons had placed in the newspapers about her escape, all while thinking about his communications with Oliver Wolcott. And, as he waited for Ona to arrive, he could have thought of the men and women who had worked for his own family as slaves—those who had been freed.

Ona would have entered his office both reserved and alert, sizing up Joseph as he started to ask her questions about sewing and cooking. She needed this job. But as his questions continued, Ona started to feel uncomfortable. Something was off. Joseph was being *too* nice to her.

In truth, Joseph was increasingly charmed by Ona.

He recognized her intelligence, but more significantly, he saw what a proud woman she was. Still, he kept asking questions. Did she have a husband? Was there someone in her life? Did she, perhaps, have a relationship with a man from France?

Ona would have been disturbed by this line of questioning. She would also have been alarmed. Joseph knew who she was. This was not a job interview; this was a white man, a slave catcher apprehending his prey. She grew quiet, and waited. The men with the strong arms and greedy eyes—those men from her nightmares—were going to enter and carry her back to slavery, back to misery.

Joseph watched Ona as she tried to hide her despair. He realized that she knew he was acting, that he had lured her to this meeting under false pretenses. The ball was in his court. Should he abide by the suggestion of the president and force her down to the shipyard and push her onto the nearest boat?

Or should he listen to his own conscience?

Joseph told Ona the truth. George Washington did know where she was. He had asked Joseph to capture her and put her on a ship. Ona must have stared at him, waiting for the inevitable chains, or ropes, or whatever restraints they used in New Hampshire.

But then Joseph surprised Ona. He said he was

ERICA ARMSTRONG DUNBAR and KATHLEEN VAN CLEVE

her ally, not her enemy. He wanted to know why she had run away. He talked about other ways she could live, alternatives to a life of enslavement. Joseph was actually *talking* to her like a human, not like property. This gave Ona courage. After gathering her thoughts, she said what she really felt. Under no circumstances would she return to slavery, where she could be "sold or given to any person."

She would rather die than return.

This was it. The moment in a human's life when all those sayings that are taught during childhood—be courageous, be smart, be kind—collided into a disgusting but legal institution called slavery that permitted some human beings to be regarded as not human at all, but property, and only because of the color of their skin. Joseph was obligated by law to return the fugitive slave to her owner. But he also knew that George was not willing to go through all the obstacles that were required by the law if he insisted on capturing Ona.

Ona and Joseph were at a crossroads. Joseph suggested a compromise. He said he would negotiate with the president about Ona's freedom in the future, after George and Martha had died. This would mean that she could return to work for the Washingtons—a much more pleasant job than the new kind of work she had to do in New Hampshire—and she wouldn't always have to look over her shoulder, fearful that she would be caught. All Ona had to do was trust him.

Ona listened to every word Joseph said. She nodded as he told her that he could almost guarantee her future freedom. She barely blinked when he reminded her that her previous work was so much easier than what she had to endure in New Hampshire. And finally, as she stood to leave, she agreed to return to the Washingtons. Joseph sat back in his chair, relieved. Ona politely said her goodbye.

And then, as Ona walked down the street, she shook her head. He had fallen for *her* trick. Ona's determination was as solid as the granite stone found underneath all of New Hampshire. She would never willingly return to slavery, promise of future freedom or not. If the president wanted to claim her, he would have to do it by force.

Of course, Joseph didn't know that. When Ona left their meeting, he probably congratulated himself for a job well done. A couple of days later, he arranged for a vessel to take Ona to Philadelphia. When it was in dock at Portsmouth, he sent word to her that it had arrived. He knew it was his responsibility to watch Ona board the ship, so he most likely paced around the dock, waiting for her to arrive. He waited and waited, perhaps checking his timepiece when it was time for

ERICA ARMSTRONG DUNBAR and KATHLEEN VAN CLEVE

the ship to depart. Joseph may have taken one last look around, realizing what had happened. Ona had played *him*. She was not going to get on that boat.

Joseph told the ship captain that he could shove off the dock and start his voyage. Despite the fact that the leader of the United States was going to be *really* ticked off—and despite the fact that Ona had definitely made life more difficult for him—he might have smiled.

When Joseph wrote about his experience with Ona to Secretary Wolcott, he was apologetic but clear. There was no Frenchman. It was only a "thirst for compleat freedom" that had driven Ona away from Philadelphia. Knowing that the Washingtons were going to be furious with her, he wrote that Ona had expressed only affection toward the president and his wife.

She expressed great affection & Reverence for her Master & Mistress, and without hesitation declared her willingness to return & to serve with fidelity during the lives of the President & his Lady if she could be freed on their decease, should she outlive them.

The only way Joseph could see Ona Judge returning to the Washingtons was if she were eventually set free. Boldly, Joseph told Oliver (who would then write to the president) that gradual emancipation—that is the gradual freeing of the slaves—was the best path for the president to take. In other words, the customs collector, Joseph Whipple, dared to tell the first president of the United States that he should consider abandoning slavery, and that he should begin with Ona Judge.

Joseph didn't stop there. He continued to write that the president should be reminded that attitudes in New Hampshire were changing every single day—and that fewer and fewer of the people of New Hampshire supported slavery. Further, neither white nor black New Hampshire citizens were likely to support the actions of a president who was breaking his own laws. Free blacks would do anything they could to keep Ona and fugitives like her from returning to slavery. Joseph wrote, "The popular opinion here in favor of universal freedom has rendered it difficult to get them back to their masters."

Joseph ended his letter with a polite request to be taken out of the whole mess. Given what he knew, from meeting directly with Ona, that there was no way she would return to slavery on her own, Joseph thought the president should hire a lawyer, who should then contact New Hampshire's own state attorney to

ERICA ARMSTRONG DUNBAR and KATHLEEN VAN CLEVE

figure out how to handle this troubling situation. In other words, if George and Martha wanted Ona back, they would have to follow the law and consequently expose themselves to the growing antislavery sentiment in New Hampshire.

Oliver Wolcott received Joseph Whipple's letter in Philadelphia. He must have read it in a state of shock; it was rare to have someone be so candid with the president of the United States. Then Oliver turned the letter over to George Washington.

It is safe to say that George was not happy. More accurately, it could be said that he went ballistic.

He picked up a pen, cut out the middleman—Oliver—and began a long letter to Joseph Whipple himself. The date was November 28. Ona had been gone for six months.

> To enter into such a compromise with her ... is totally inadmissible ... for however well disposed I might be to a gradual abolition, or even to an entire emancipation of that description of people (if the latter was in itself practicable at this moment) it would neither be politic or just, to reward unfaithfulness with a premature preference.

This part of his letter reflected George Washington's own conflicted feelings about slavery. When combined with letters George Washington wrote to Tobias Lear and the Marquis de Lafayette, it is clear that he was increasingly uneasy about human bondage.

At the same time, Ona had clearly crossed the line. She had disrespected him and his wife. He was offended by the very idea of negotiating with a slave. In his mind, Ona's conduct was indefensible, and he would not reward her bad behavior with the promise of freedom. Instead he told Joseph to assure Ona that she "will be forgiven by her Mistress; and she will meet with the same treatment from me, that all the rest of her family (which is a very numerous one) shall receive."

On the surface this seems like George was telling Joseph to tell Ona that everything would be the same as before. This was really a way to threaten all of Ona's relatives at Mount Vernon with pain and suffering because of Ona's actions. This was the only way George would negotiate with Ona. If she didn't come back, her family could be hurt.

George wasn't finished. He said that if Ona continued to refuse to return voluntarily, Joseph should place her on a vessel headed for Alexandria, Virginia, or the new Federal City—in other words, directly back into the jaws of slavery. He did not want Joseph to use extreme force,

ERICA ARMSTRONG DUNBAR and KATHLEEN VAN CLEVE

because this could "excite a mob or riot." He was too close to the end of his presidency for a scandal like that. Instead Joseph should use discretion. If done properly, Ona could be back to the Washingtons fairly quickly. This was something he wished for his wife, he wrote, who was "desirous of receiving her again."

George ended the letter with a statement that was both strange and 100 percent false:

> We had vastly rather she should be sent to Virginia than brought to this place [Philadelphia]; as our stay here will be but short; and as it is not unlikely that she may, from the circumstances I have mentioned, be in a state of pregnancy.

No one has any idea why George believed that Ona was pregnant. She wasn't. Perhaps George was more dramatically inclined than he seemed. Or maybe he still could not conceive of a world where a young woman would want to leave his home so much that she risked everything, including the well-being of her family, to get away. There is one final possibility. We do know that because Ona was considered property, any child of hers would also become the property of the Washingtons. If she was pregnant, Ona's value would increase, and she and her unborn child would be worth more money.

Of course, this is speculation of an alternative fact; there was no pregnancy.

Joseph must have read and reread this letter for days on end. It took him almost a month to respond. In his reply, dated December 22, he was precise with his words. He needed to convey that he had worked very hard to protect the president's reputation, while at the same time attempting to get Ona to return to Mount Vernon without abiding by the regulations of the Fugitive Slave Act. In other words, he wrote that he had done what he could to help George break his own law without letting the public know. He agreed, halfheartedly, to pursue Ona as long as there was no public attention given to the matter. And then Joseph closed his letter with an extraordinary piece of political advice for the most respected man in the country. Joseph suggested that gradual emancipation of all slaves would be the only way to stop the tide of fugitives. Slave owners like George Washington could "prevent this growing evil"—all they had to do was free their slaves.

It is hard to imagine the relief Joseph must have felt when he sent the letter off to the president.

George Washington never wrote back. Perhaps he

accepted that his influence over the customs collector was far less than he had anticipated. The United States of America, still very young, was growing up. The conflicts between the states in the North and the South were not going away. George Washington had served his country for decades, but as he was resigning from the presidency and public life, he had to also acknowledge that the country, like any child, would continue to grow and change whether he liked its decisions or not. Right now George had to put country first—before the desires of his wife and before his own anger at Ona. He had to turn his attention to the peaceful transfer of power from himself to John Adams, his Massachusetts-born vice president, who had just weeks before narrowly won the first contested American presidential election against Thomas Jefferson, Thomas Pinckney, and Aaron Burr.

Ona Judge was safe, for now.

CHAPTER TWENTY-TWO
MRS. STAINES

THREE DAYS AFTER JOSEPH WHIPPLE PENNED HIS LETTER to the president, Ona celebrated her first Christmas away from the Washingtons. She would not have had enough money to buy expensive gifts for her new friends in Portsmouth, but she may have given them nuts or a small amount of chocolate to thank them for all they had done for her. It had been a terrifying, exhilarating, gratifying year. For the rest of her life, she would always worry about the relatives she had left at Mount Vernon. She would always be worried about being captured. But Joseph Whipple had been correct when he'd said that Ona had a "thirst for complete freedom." The fact that she found herself in Portsmouth, New Hampshire, earning money for her work, choosing to make everyday decisions that free people often took for granted, would have seemed unbelievable to her, except that it was indeed true.

Ona was also allowed, for the first time, to control her personal life. This meant that like many other free men and women, she was able to consider forming her own family, on her own terms. And Ona had, in her short time in Portsmouth, found the person she wanted to spend her life with: a free black sailor named Jack Staines.

It is kind of funny to think about George Washington's claims that Ona had been scorned by a French boyfriend who had abandoned her when she was pregnant, when in truth she had met the person she wanted to share her life with, someone whom she had met and chosen after she had made her momentous decision to run away. Ona had waited long enough. She wanted a husband.

The truth was, she also *needed* a husband.

Living alone was not easy in early America, especially for a black woman fugitive. Today we like to believe that most people get to choose their romantic partner, and moreover, that they make that choice because they are in love with their partner. But in early America, men and women across the new nation sometimes married for reasons other than love. Often they married just in order to survive. A young male farmer might marry a woman because her father had promised the farmer some money or property (called a dowry) if the farmer married his daughter. When the couple had children, they would grow up to assist their fathers and mothers in the fields, in the home, or in their line of work if they weren't farmers, continuing the cycle.

Ona did not have a dowry, but she was young and healthy. It's impossible to know if she and Jack wanted to get married for convenience, love, or something in between. Whatever the reason, Ona Judge began 1797 with a legal marriage to a free black man whom she had chosen, without any outside influence. Less than one year earlier, Ona had been told that she would be a wedding gift, and she knew that in Virginia, she would never experience a legal marriage. This was a remarkable leap of circumstances for a young woman in an extremely short period of time.

Jack Staines was like many other free black men who lived along the Eastern Seaboard, choosing to spend long periods of time working at sea. Black men who did this were called "black jacks," and although this line of work was not seen as proper for white men, it offered opportunity to black men who couldn't find a decent-paying job elsewhere. It wasn't that black men

ERICA ARMSTRONG DUNBAR and KATHLEEN VAN CLEVE

were not the targets of racism when they were at sea—they absolutely were—but the position was still seen as preferable to being on the streets, where corrupt slave catchers and kidnappers lurked to take free black men away and sell them into southern slavery.

Additionally, many black sailors were often catapulted into positions of honor in early free black communities, receiving equal pay with the white sailors on their voyages. Often the lump-sum payments that Jack Staines and other black seafaring men received when they returned home from their journeys were used to buy land or even a home—an unreachable goal for most black men at the end of the 1700s.

Ona knew that being married to a black sailor would be filled with opportunities. She had found someone who could help provide for her and whatever children they might have together. Yet she also knew that marriage to a sailor would mean long absences and weeks of staying home alone. On his side, Jack was almost certainly aware that Ona was a fugitive and thus legally the property of Martha Washington. But whatever the disadvantages to their union, Ona and Jack wanted to be married, legally, in front of their friends and certified by the government.

Jack and Ona celebrated Christmas in 1796 by visiting the county clerk in Portsmouth, where they applied for a marriage certificate. They were careful to follow the law, to be certain that their marriage was legally recognized by the state. This was important symbolically but also practically. If something happened to Jack at sea and Ona was his legal wife, she would be able to receive any money owed to Jack or any land he had purchased.

It would have been a happy story if they had been able to get the approval without any problems, but life was never going to be easy for Ona. Joseph Whipple had heard through the grapevine about Ona's marriage plans, and despite his respect for Ona, he felt it was his duty to tell the Portsmouth county clerk that she was a fugitive, owned by the president's family. Their paperwork was delayed, and soon the county clerk advised the couple that getting a marriage certificate in Portsmouth was impossible.

What we know from this is twofold. One: Ona and Jack did not give up. And two: Joseph Whipple, while remaining truthful, again allowed Ona to live as a free person by not forcing her return to the Washingtons.

Ona and Jack must have asked around, collected advice, and figured out a way to get what they wanted. They traveled to a smaller nearby town, Greenland, five miles from Portsmouth, where they filled out the documents for county clerk Thomas Philbrook. On

ERICA ARMSTRONG DUNBAR and KATHLEEN VAN CLEVE

the very same day that George Washington's Farewell Address was printed on the first page of the *New-Hampshire Gazette*—January 14, 1797—the news of Ona Judge's marriage to Jack Staines also appeared in the newspaper. A simple ten words publicly announced their union: "In this town, Mr. John Staines, to Miss Oney Judge."

Samuel Haven, reverend of Portsmouth's South Church, married them. The exact details are unknown, but we can guess that Ona would have pulled out one of her nicer dresses, one that she may have worn while serving Martha. A veil would have been too expensive and impractical. Jack probably would have dressed in a tailcoat (a men's dress coat with longer fabric in the back) and his nicest pair of trousers. There wouldn't have been a fancy reception, but they may have shared a simple dinner common for the time: fish or oyster stew, brown bread, and maybe a bit of Indian pudding for dessert.

Ona became Ona Staines. The two of them, we can hope, lived a life of domestic contentment—at least when Jack was not at sea. We know from the New Hampshire census in 1800 that Jack Staines was listed as the head of household, along with three other people in the Staines home. What is noteworthy about this entry is that no slaves were recorded as living in this home, which meant that Ona was passing as a free woman. Early census records offered lots of details for white families, such as the gender and age of all the household occupants. This was not the same for people of color. It was only noted whether the inhabitants were free, and the total number of people living in the home.

We do not know who the other two people were who lived with Ona and Jack, but we can safely assume that at least one of these other housemates was someone in need, just like Ona had been when she'd first arrived in Portsmouth. It was common for poor families to house boarders in their homes if there was room, because it meant extra money for household expenses. For Ona and Jack this extra money would come at a perfect time because Ona was expecting a child.

Ona would have still continued to work as long as she could while she was pregnant, even scrubbing floors and lifting heavy containers of water despite her growing belly. But eventually, sometime in 1798, Ona gave birth to a healthy baby girl. They named her Eliza, the same name as the woman who had basically triggered Ona's entire escape from slavery.

It is worthwhile to stop and consider what a massive political and personal achievement the birth of Eliza Staines was for Ona. She had been able to choose her husband, marry him legally, and have a child when she wanted to have a child. She was able to raise Eliza in the way that she and Jack desired. She did not have to rush back to work in the President's House to sew dresses, as Betty had done for Martha Washington when Ona was born, and Ona did not have to automatically leave Eliza with caregivers from sunup to sundown as enslaved mothers often had to do.

At the same time, Ona never forgot that she was still a fugitive. Worse: according to the current law, she had passed the disease of slavery to her daughter. Even though Eliza had been born in Portsmouth, and even though Jack Staines was a legally free black man, Ona's status as enslaved meant that Eliza, too, if captured, would be considered enslaved. The pressure on Ona to protect her daughter made her even more determined to never, ever be caught.

CHAPTER TWENTY-THREE

ONE LAST TRY

BY 1799 ONA AND JACK STAINES AND THEIR BABY, ELIZA, appear to have been living as happily as possible in Portsmouth, New Hampshire. Always poor and always working, they managed to find a way to pursue life, liberty, and happiness.

At the same time, George and Martha Washington had still not gotten over the fact that they had been unable to capture Ona Judge. Now the retired gentleman farmer at Mount Vernon that he had always wanted to be, George Washington—perhaps with a nudge from Martha—rekindled his mission of getting Ona to return to Mount Vernon, where he was certain she belonged.

The person George chose to carry out this job was Martha's nephew Burwell Bassett Jr. Burwell was thirty-five years old, nine years older than Ona. He had known Ona as a child, from his visits to Mount Vernon. Now he was a member of the Virginia Senate. George thought this would give Burwell an excuse to travel to New Hampshire and tell people he was there "for business."

George instructed Burwell to meet with John Langdon after arriving in New Hampshire. It had not occurred to George that John would no longer be his ally in his quest to retake Ona. But times had continued to change, and George had still not fully taken into account how much attitudes toward slavery were shifting, particularly with politicians such as John. For example, John had officially switched political parties, moving from the Federalists (George Washington's party) to the Democratic-Republicans (the political party headed, at the time, by Thomas Jefferson). George ignored this. It seemed that he was the only person unable to get over the past: Ona had been gone for almost three years, yet he was determined to get her back. He was certain John Langdon would support him in this venture, and he insisted on continuing his absurd claim that Ona had been "enticed away by a Frenchman." In the same stubborn spirit, he also maintained his position that he would not allow Ona to negotiate for her own freedom, writing that it would set a "dangerous precedent."

Burwell Bassett set out for New Hampshire and did indeed stay with the Langdons during his time in Portsmouth. Burwell discovered that not only had John Langdon switched political parties, but he had publicly expressed reservations about including slavery in the US Constitution. All the Langdon family slaves had been freed and then rehired as paid laborers. Despite all this, Burwell could not believe that John Langdon would not help him and his uncle George in their effort to capture Ona. After all, Burwell reasoned, John did not refer to himself as a leader in the early antislavery movement. When Burwell arrived in Portsmouth, he must have assumed it would be a relatively easy day's work to grab Ona, put her on a ship, and sail back to Virginia. After all, he knew exactly where she was.

Burwell went to Ona's house shortly after his arrival. We can imagine this moment. Ona, now about twenty-six, hears a knock on the door. Baby Eliza, now about one year old, would be close by her, toddling around on unsteady legs. Jack Staines was away at sea. Ona was used to Jack's travel schedule and was just happy contemplating the day when he was scheduled to return. The knock on the door could have been anyone: a free black friend, a white friend, someone who wanted Ona to watch their child while they left to do an errand.

So Ona opens the door. And then, instead of a friend, she sees her nightmares come to life. Standing in front of her is a man she recognizes from her youth. George and Martha have not given up. They are still after her.

Fear clenches her heart. Instinctively she picks up Eliza and holds her close as she faces Burwell Bassett Jr. for the first time in years. How she wishes that she hadn't answered the door.

Burwell follows the script that George suggested to him before he left Mount Vernon. If Ona voluntarily returns to Virginia, she will not face any punishment for her misdeeds. Burwell does his best not to speak to her harshly, but it would be better, and more truthful, if he did, because Burwell has every intention of treating Ona and her daughter roughly if he has to.

"Will you come with me?" he may have said, as politely as he could.

Ona stares at him, her little girl's warm body fueling her courage. After what probably seems like a very long time, Ona answers Burwell very simply.

"No."

As a native southerner, Burwell would have been offended to his core that he had to negotiate with this woman, this slave. Yet it becomes clear, quickly, that Ona is not going to budge.

Burwell swallows his anger and sweetens the deal, promising that the Washingtons "would set her free when she arrived at Mount Vernon." Ona knows this is a lie, but she stands there and listens. Perhaps Burwell continues with promises for an easy, non-dramatic return to the estate—maybe even reminding Ona of her family still living at Mount Vernon, or how Martha is still just plain devastated at Ona's loss, because there is no one who is as wonderful as her best slave. Ona is missed! Ona is needed!

Maybe Burwell looks around at that moment and delivers his strongest argument. If she goes with him, Ona and Eliza will not have to live in poverty in New Hampshire.

As Burwell prattles on, Ona finds her resolve. When he finally finishes speaking, she looks him straight in the eyes. Her response is final, and fierce.

"I am free now and choose to remain so."

CHAPTER TWENTY-FOUR
GREENLAND

FOR BURWELL BASSETT JR., THIS TRIP TO ONA'S HOUSE had turned his world upside down. He was stunned. Ona was not free, legally, but he knew now that this was going to be a bigger fight than he'd expected. They must have stared at each other, Ona holding her baby, righteous in her stance; and Burwell, cascades of mixed-up thoughts about slavery coursing through his mind. After a long moment of silence, he probably doffed his hat and walked away from the Staineses' home.

After this terrifying visit, Ona was more resolved than ever to protect her daughter and herself with all her might.

Burwell was growing angrier with every step he took back to the Langdons'. He understood that northern sentiment about slavery was different from in the South, but Ona's clear belief that she was *equal* to him had ignited his own temper. In Virginia, if a slave ever talked to her owner the way Ona had spoken to Burwell, she would be swiftly and severely punished. Burwell's southern manners hid a rigid sense of how he felt personally insulted. Ona had not seen the last of him.

Back at the Langdons' house, Burwell told the senator that Ona had refused to return to Virginia. By this time Burwell had mentally regrouped. He would not leave the fugitive slave in Portsmouth, no matter what.

Senator John Langdon was in a difficult position. As an elected official, he was obligated to follow the laws of the land, which at this time still included the returning of fugitives across state lines. But outside of his own personal moral beliefs, this was a delicate situation, one that required the senator to walk a fragile line between obeying federal law and abiding by the growing anti-slavery position of his state's citizens.

As Ona's fate was up in the air, secret and unknown allies came to her aid once again. Someone told Ona that Burwell was going to come back to her house and take her and Eliza by force to a boat. This could have

ERICA ARMSTRONG DUNBAR and KATHLEEN VAN CLEVE

been Senator Langdon himself or, more likely, one of his free black servants. Either way, the news that Burwell was going to return to her home was relayed to Ona almost immediately.

During the next day, Burwell most likely notified a few friends who he knew could be discreet and who could help contain Ona and Eliza if she resisted. Burwell would have hoped to avoid a scene because of the potential for public attention, but he was prepared. If Ona continued to be so resistant, he and his friends would have no choice but to tie up her arms and legs, gag the baby, and forcibly place the mother and child in the back of a wagon.

In his mind, he was fighting not only for George and Martha, but for the South itself. It's almost certain that a ship was already stationed in port and ready to sail directly to Alexandria, Virginia. All Burwell had to do was get Ona there.

Burwell arrived at Ona's house and knocked at the door, probably politely at first. His friends would have been nearby, waiting. There was no answer. He knocked again, a bit more heatedly. Still no answer. Eventually Burwell forced his way into Ona's home.

No one was there. Ona and Eliza had disappeared.

There were no telephones or cars or GPS to try to track Ona down. Burwell himself had no relationships with the free black community in Portsmouth; there was no one to give him any hints as to where Ona could have gone. It was a rural state where the places available for Ona to vanish seemed infinite. Burwell had failed, and failed spectacularly.

What had happened was that when Ona had learned of Burwell's plans to forcibly return her to Virginia, she'd gone to a nearby farm and hired a stableboy to use a horse and carriage to carry Eliza and her to nearby Greenland, the town five miles away from Portsmouth where she and Jack had been married. The stableboy drove the carriage to the home of a free black family headed by Phillis and John Jack, who opened their home to Ona and Eliza. It was one of countless acts of selflessness and humane behavior during a time when the laws did not match up with the ideals of the young country. It was also, on Ona's part, just another example of heroic, courageous behavior that had evolved because of the most fundamental of pursuits: the pursuit of freedom.

CHAPTER TWENTY-FIVE

THE WASHINGTONS

ON DECEMBER 12, 1799, GEORGE WASHINGTON TOOK WHAT was a routine horseback ride around Mount Vernon. He spent much of the day outside, even as it snowed and hailed and rained. Returning home later than he expected, he refused to be late to dinner, so he joined his family and ate in his wet riding clothes. Throughout the evening, snow continued to accumulate on his estate, and George Washington began to get sick. Initially it was a sore throat, which grew worse, causing swelling around his vocal cords and a raspy voice. He had to cut short his nightly ritual of reading the newspaper before retiring to bed.

Sleep didn't come. Martha wanted to call the doctor,

but George refused. They waited until their house slave Caroline lit the fireplace at daybreak before they sent for assistance. Tobias Lear was the first to arrive, and he was alarmed to find George extremely ill and struggling to breathe. A home remedy of molasses, butter, and vinegar was mixed together and given to George to soothe his sore throat. But the mixture was so thick that it was almost impossible for George to swallow, and he almost suffocated.

Dr. James Craik, a physician and longtime friend of the Washingtons, arrived next. James and two other physicians tried everything they could, but it was clear the situation was getting worse, not better. In what seemed like a superhuman effort, George asked for Martha to come to his bedside and bring with her two wills that he had stored in his study. He was able to review each of them, and when he was finished, he handed her one will and told her to burn the other in the fire. Then he called for Tobias Lear. Still able to speak, George was very clear about his last wishes:

> *I find I am going, my breath cannot last long. I believed from the first that the disorder would prove fatal. . . . Arrange my accounts and settle my books, as you know more about them than anyone else.*

ERICA ARMSTRONG DUNBAR and KATHLEEN VAN CLEVE

George Washington died on December 14, 1799. Surrounding him were Martha Washington, his friends and doctors, and four slaves.

The will that George had handed to Martha revealed a man who had indeed struggled with the concept of slavery. In his will George stated that all 123 slaves that he had owned directly were to be freed upon the death of his wife, Martha. He had considered freeing them immediately upon his own death, but he had changed his mind, stating that this would actually cause hardship for the enslaved families at Mount Vernon because all the other slaves there—153 of them—were controlled by Martha Washington through the estate of her deceased first husband, Daniel Parke Custis. Many of the slaves at Mount Vernon had intermarried. According to George, the immediate release of his slaves would cause "disagreeable consequences" among the families who were composed of slaves owned by George and slaves owned by the Custis estate. In other words, there would be free and enslaved people in one family, which he thought would cause problems.

George surprised many with the conditions he set forth for both his aged slaves and younger slaves whose parents were deceased. For the aged slaves—those who could not work or support themselves—he required that they be "comfortably clothed and fed" even after they were freed. The younger slaves were to work as servants until they were twenty-five, but during that time they were "to be taught to read & write: and to be brought up to some useful occupation."

The only slave who was immediately emancipated in George's will was his faithful valet, William Lee. William had the option to remain enslaved (so that he would not have to find a new job with wages) or be free immediately. But it was clearly stated in the will that William Lee could make this decision on his own and that in either situation, he would receive thirty dollars a year, along with food and clothing.

George did this, he wrote, "as a testimony of my sense of his attachment to me, and for his faithful services during the Revolutionary War."

William Lee died during the winter of 1810 and was buried in the slave burial ground at Mount Vernon.

Martha, though grieving the loss of George, was almost immediately aware that the only thing standing in the way of freedom for 123 slaves was the fact that she was still alive. She began to be afraid that the almost-freed slaves would kill her. She confided this fear to her friend, Abigail Adams, the wife of the current president, John Adams.

Abigail wrote, "She did not feel as tho her Life was

ERICA ARMSTRONG DUNBAR and KATHLEEN VAN CLEVE

safe in their Hands," because she was afraid that the slaves, "would be told that it was [in] their interest to get rid of her." Martha's anxiety grew when a series of suspicious events occurred throughout 1800, especially a large fire set in one of Mount Vernon's buildings. It was the final straw, and Martha knew she couldn't wait until she died to free George's slaves. She amended George's will, and his slaves were set free on January 1, 1801.

Back in New Hampshire, Ona would have certainly learned about the death of the first president of the United States. Her own anxiety about being caught, however, would not have lessened. Ona always knew she was technically owned by Martha and her heirs, not George directly, and as a result, she was still legally their property. Ona also knew that Martha would never relinquish her slaves or encourage her grandchildren to free theirs. Even when Martha died in May 1802, Ona understood that legally speaking, she was not now and never would be free. But in her soul, she knew she was.

CHAPTER TWENTY-SIX

THE SURVIVOR

IF THIS STORY WERE FICTION, THIS WOULD BE THE TIME to say that Ona lived happily ever after. George and Martha had both died and she was living in faraway New Hampshire. But this story is not fiction, and while Ona definitely had happy moments, the rest of her life in New Hampshire was filled with immense hardship.

We know from census records and the interviews Ona gave to journalists at the end of her life that she had two more children after Eliza: William, born in 1800, and Nancy, born in 1802. Ona continued to navigate her way through the joys of parenthood, marriage, and life outside of slavery during the very early

1800s. But she and Jack were constantly dealing with the same realities of poverty that Ona had witnessed when she'd worked with the white servants in New York City, when George Washington was first elected president. There was never enough money. Ona would work as a maid in homes as much as she could, while still making sure her small children were cared for. Jack would spend days and weeks and months away on sea voyages in order to be given that lump-sum payment that was so necessary for his family to survive.

When Jack died in 1803, Ona had—again—to reach back into her reservoir of strength and figure out a way to keep her family alive. There is no information about the circumstances of Jack's death; we just know that his death notice appeared in the *New-Hampshire Gazette* on May 3, 1803.

Ona first had an opportunity to work for a neighboring family, the Bartletts, but she turned down the job when she discovered that she could not bring along her young children. She would have looked for other jobs, but the same problem would have persisted: people wanted maids, not maids with babies tagging along. Ona decided to turn back to the family that had sheltered her and Eliza when Burwell Bassett, the nephew of the Washingtons, had showed up on her doorstep—the Jacks.

This was the family who had opened their doors to Ona and Eliza in 1799. Phillis Jack was the matriarch of the family and—in a surprising turn of events—the owner of both the home and the land on which it stood. Land ownership was very rare, especially for free black women. Phillis had been given the home by her former slave owner, the religious Deacon James Brackett, who had freed her in the 1760s. Often a white owner who had become excessively fond of a black female slave gave her a home so that he could always see her when he wished, and perhaps this is what happened between Deacon Brackett and Phillis Jack. Alternatively, Deacon Brackett could have chosen a more uncommon path: he could have given Phillis Jack the land and the home, with no strings attached, just out of the goodness of his heart. The end result was that Phillis and her family lived in a home that straddled the border between Greenland and Stratham, New Hampshire. Phillis's husband was called by many names: Jack Warner (the last name of his former slave owner), John Jack, Black Jack, and Jacks. He had earned his freedom by serving in the Revolutionary War. Phillis and John had two daughters: Nancy and Phillis.

Now, in 1803, Ona moved back to the house with her three children. But tragedy struck again when

Phillis died in October 1804, just a year after Ona's husband, Jack Staines, had passed away. Despite owning the home, the Jack and Staines families had become almost completely penniless, with not enough money to give Phillis an honorable funeral. Luckily, private citizens stepped in to cover the cost of the burial.

The two families merged and scraped together as much money as they could to keep a roof over their heads, food in their bellies, and clothes on their backs. But like other struggling black families, it proved impossible. Ona had to agree to let her daughters, Eliza and Nancy, move to the nearby farm of Nathan Johnson for eight months. In return for providing food and shelter for Eliza and Nancy, Nathan would receive thirty-five dollars from the town government. Ona's daughters would be put to work in the fields and in the home as servants to the six members of the Johnson family. It was probably around this same time—1816— that Ona and Jack's only son, William, left to become a sailor. Life in Greenland had become too difficult for him, and despite Ona's best efforts to clothe and feed him, William knew he had to set off on his own. He left Greenland for the seaports along the East Coast and was never again recorded as a New Hampshire resident. Ona was now living in the Jack home with Nancy and Phillis Jack and their father, John Jack.

By 1817, John Jack had died too. Eliza and Nancy had returned, but the house seemed to be an inescapable place of misery. All five women did odd jobs, domestic work, and anything to bring in additional income. Both Nancy and Eliza Staines had become known for their artistic ability, and as they grew into adulthood, they began to sell their sketches to wealthy Portsmouth families. This definitely helped. But the one practical method that women of this and all time periods had often used to ensure stability—marriage—evaded the women in the Jack home. Ona did not remarry, and none of the younger women—Nancy and Eliza Staines and Phillis and Nancy Jack—ever married at all. Over the next several years of the antebellum period, little changed for the women except that the small house began to show signs of aging. The women who lived there were just happy to have a roof over their heads; poverty's roots were too deep.

More suffering lay in wait for Ona. No parent ever wants to outlive their children, but that was Ona's fate. Eliza succumbed to a long illness on February 16, 1832, when she was thirty-four, and Nancy died the following year, on September 11, 1833, also from an illness. Immediate and useful medical care was still a haphazard business in the early 1800s, particularly for women who were as poor as Ona, Eliza, and Nancy.

ERICA ARMSTRONG DUNBAR and KATHLEEN VAN CLEVE

The three women had experienced lives filled with challenges, concerns about hunger, forced servitude, and the ever-present fear of slave catchers. Ona had done the best she could, but now, in her late fifties, she was once again alone.

Ona had been through so much. She had made heroic decisions and stood up to the most powerful man in the country. And yet she was confronted constantly with the loss of the people who meant the most to her. It was ultimately her faith in God and a fervent conversion to Christianity that carried Ona Maria Judge Staines through the most difficult periods of her life.

When she had escaped to New Hampshire, Ona had begun attending Reverend Samuel Haven's South Church in Portsmouth. Later she became a Baptist, after hearing the sermons of Elias Smith, a traveling preacher who moved to Portsmouth in 1802. Once she'd moved in with the Jack family, Ona probably attended the Baptist church in Stratham, only a mile's walk from her home. At some point during her time in New Hampshire, she had learned to read. This would have put Ona on the same path as many other free African Americans, whose literacy rates climbed during the first half of the nineteenth century. She read the Bible over and over again, believing its central creed that she would see her beloved family again in heaven.

Decades later it was probably Ona's connection to the Baptist church in Stratham that brought Reverend Thomas Archibald to Ona's doorstep. Reverend Thomas Archibald asked to interview Ona about her past, for an abolitionist newspaper called the *Granite Freeman*. At this time, in 1845, Ona was close to seventy-three years old. She was finally ready to talk; it was almost forty-nine years to the day since she had escaped from Philadelphia.

In the interview in the *Granite Freeman* and in a later interview with the abolitionist newspaper the *Liberator*, once again, Ona told the world her story. A week after her interview with the *Granite Freeman* was published, the paper announced the publication of a new autobiography, called *Narrative of the Life of Frederick Douglass, an American Slave*. Douglass, another fugitive, became world-famous for his brilliant writing and activism for the equality of all African Americans.

With Ona's children deceased, and her advanced age keeping her from being pulled back into slavery, she was no longer fearful of being returned to the Custis heirs. She answered Reverend Archibald's questions with honesty and "a smile that played upon

ERICA ARMSTRONG DUNBAR and KATHLEEN VAN CLEVE

her withered countenance." She questioned George Washington's religious practice and went on to say that "Mrs. Washington used to *read* prayers but I don't call that praying." When asked if she was sorry to have left the Washingtons, particularly because her life had been so difficult and sorrow-filled since she'd escaped to New Hampshire, she replied with strength and the calm wisdom of a woman who'd had the courage to do what was morally right: "No, I am free, and have, I trust, been made a child of God by the means."

Ona's interview in the *Liberator* on January 1, 1847, introduced her story to thousands of readers across the nation, permanently linking her to the crusade for black freedom in the years leading up to the Civil War. A little over a year later, in February 1848, a doctor named George Odell paid a call to the Jack household, where only Nancy Jack and Ona Staines resided. Dr. Odell's house call was most likely to treat Ona, now close to seventy-five years old. But whatever cures or treatment he may have prescribed were unsuccessful.

On February 25, 1848, eleven days after the doctor's visit, Ona Maria Judge Staines was carried away, not by slave catchers, but by her God.

ONA MARIA JUDGE STAINES HAD NO REGRETS. DESPITE the poverty, despite the sorrow, despite the permanent, painful separation from her family, Ona spent her final fifty years on earth living in a freedom of her own making—a freedom that allowed her to marry the man of her choice, bear children when she wanted to have children, and get paid for her labor. For some of this period, she must have experienced a joy from marriage and family and faith that she would never have imagined possible. The painful times of her life were set against the happy triumphs of her self-made freedom; her daring escape in 1796 had opened a door she never wanted closed again.

Yet as this door remained open for Ona, it closed, at least in the short term, for people near to her. The summer of 1796 was not a happy one for Martha Washington. Not only did she have to return to Mount Vernon without Ona attending to her every need, she had to do so knowing that Ona had publicly, stunningly, chosen a life on the run rather than stay another second serving Martha and her family. Martha was angry because she wholeheartedly believed she had treated Ona more like a family member than a servant. In Martha's opinion, Ona not only should not have had the audacity to run away—she should have been grateful to Martha for her "good" treatment!

Indeed, Martha's sense that Ona was the epitome of ungrateful was foreshadowed almost an exact year before the escape, in a letter she wrote to her niece, Fanny Bassett Washington, Burwell's sister. "Blacks are so bad in their nature," Martha wrote, "that they have not the least gratitude for the kindness that may be showed to them."

The news of Ona's escape would have lit a fire in the souls of the enslaved at Mount Vernon. She was not only a hero; she was *their* hero. Martha would have known this, and it would have made her even more enraged. Worse, Ona's escape had left Martha in a predicament:

ERICA ARMSTRONG DUNBAR and KATHLEEN VAN CLEVE

Eliza Custis Law, her bratty granddaughter, was now married and pregnant. Eliza and her husband, Thomas, were slated to move to the Federal City in 1797. Martha felt under even more pressure to find her granddaughter another human "wedding gift."

Looking around the enslaved population at her home, Martha soon came up with the perfect substitute. She found a young enslaved woman who had spent her entire life at Mount Vernon; someone who, like Ona, was a quick learner and who seemed to have a natural grace about her that would make her able to deal with Eliza's moods.

The person? Ona's little sister, sixteen-year-old Philadelphia. If choosing Ona's sister to be Eliza's wedding gift also meant that Martha could get back at Ona for leaving her—well, that was an added bonus.

Of course, back in New Hampshire, Ona had no idea what Martha was planning. Telephones would not be invented until 1876; computers weren't invented until 1946. In early America the newspaper, handwritten letters, and old-fashioned face-to-face conversations were the ways to learn any news, family or otherwise. Ona would have learned about the major news events of the time: when George Washington gave his Farewell Address, when John Adams was elected to the presidency, when George Washington died in 1799.

Ona's contact with her own family at Mount Vernon would have ceased as soon as she stepped onto the *Nancy* and headed to New Hampshire. She would have been devastated to learn that Philadelphia was being forced to go with Eliza and Thomas Law to the Federal City. But what Ona could not know—and neither could Martha, or George, or even Philadelphia—was that the freedom Ona had so courageously grabbed for herself was soon going to show its shining face to Philadelphia, too.

Eliza Custis Law gave birth to her daughter, Elizabeth Parke Custis Law, on January 19, 1797. Soon after, she and Thomas Law moved from Mount Vernon to Georgetown, one of the two established towns in the Federal City. By this point the Federal City had been named for George Washington, with its official location called Washington, District of Columbia (or Washington, DC, as it is known today). Georgetown was located at the southern tip of Washington, DC, and was considered more remote than its twin city nine miles away, Alexandria, Virginia.

Ona's sister, Philadelphia, now seventeen, moved with the Laws. Like countless slaves before her, she had no say in these major transitions in her life, and she left her siblings and extended family at Mount

Vernon, unsure whether she would ever see them again. Still, there was one person from Mount Vernon whom she did see again. Someone who was very much a part of Martha Washington's family and someone who swung open that great door of freedom so recently pushed wide by Ona herself.

This person was William Costin.

William Costin had met Philadelphia at Mount Vernon. (He probably knew Ona, too.) He was of mixed race himself but never appeared on the slave registry at Mount Vernon because of his unique, and some would say shocking, heritage. It was believed that Martha Washington's father, John Dandridge, fathered a daughter with an enslaved woman who was of Native American and African descent. This daughter was named Ann, and she had grown up with her presumed half sister, Martha, on the Dandridge estate in New Kent County, Virginia. William Costin was Ann Dandridge's son. William Costin's father was never confirmed, but several oral histories state that his father was none other than Jacky Custis, Martha's son by her first marriage. If these accounts are accurate, then William Costin was Martha Washington's nephew *and* her grandson.

William Costin moved to Georgetown sometime in the early 1800s, after the death of Martha

Washington on May 22, 1802. At that time Martha's family and friends and much of the public mourned her death. The enslaved men and women at Mount Vernon were terrified. This was the day of reckoning; the slaves that Martha had held ownership over during her lifetime were now going to become the property of her Parke Custis grandchildren.

Even if she had wanted to free these slaves upon her death, she could not, as they had never been hers to free. Because Martha's first husband had died without a will, the law stated that all of the property that belonged to Daniel Parke Custis would automatically go to his heirs. Martha was to use these slaves during her lifetime, and upon her death, because all of her children had died, the slaves were to be turned over to her grandchildren. She saw no reason to contest this law, because it was the perfect way to keep great wealth in the family. Martha had benefited from slave labor, and so would her beloved grandchildren. The slaves remaining at Mount Vernon knew it was entirely possible that their families were going to be broken apart when the grandchildren took over their property.

There were four Parke Custis grandchildren. The oldest, Eliza Law, inherited forty-three slaves, including Philadelphia. (She was valued at eighty British

ERICA ARMSTRONG DUNBAR and KATHLEEN VAN CLEVE

pounds.) The second oldest, Martha Custis Peter, inherited forty-eight enslaved people. Nelly Custis Lewis, one of the grandchildren raised by George and Martha, was given thirty-three slaves, and "Washy"— George Washington Parke Custis—was bequeathed thirty-six. Through some stroke of providence, much of Ona's family was able to remain intact, as they were all assigned to Washy. By 1802, Washy lived at a home in Arlington, Virginia. (His home is now the site of Arlington National Cemetery.) Ona's oldest sister, Betty Davis, was able to move there with her three daughters: Nancy, Oney, and Lucinda. Ona's sister-in-law, Charlotte (Austin's widow), managed to keep her sons, Billy and Tim, and her daughters, Elvey and Eliza, by her side.

It is unclear exactly why William Costin chose Georgetown as his home. Perhaps it was because it was obvious that the nation's new capital, Washington, DC, was a fertile place for people who were intelligent and visionary, like him. Or perhaps it was because Costin's home state of Virginia was wrestling more painfully than ever with slavery. The time between the end of the Revolutionary War and the beginning of the American Civil War was a long, drawn-out battle between the quest for freedom for enslaved black Americans and the desire of many white Americans to maintain the institution of slavery, particularly in the South.

Added to this explosive mix was a spirit of rebellion—a spirit left over from the Revolutionary War but also related to the slave revolt in Haiti and a failed slave uprising in nearby Richmond, Virginia.

In 1800 there were close to two thousand black residents in Georgetown, of which about three hundred were free. Three hundred fifty free blacks lived in Alexandria. Mount Vernon was only about twenty miles south of Washington, DC, but during this unsettled time, Costin may have felt that Georgetown, across the Potomac from Virginia, was a more welcoming place for a free black man.

It is also entirely possible that William Costin chose to move to Georgetown because he was following his heart. Sometime before 1807, William Costin married Ona's sister Philadelphia, even though he was free and she was still enslaved.

Ona never knew this, but it seems as if Philadelphia and William Costin enjoyed a happy marriage that lasted more than twenty-five years and produced eight children. This was in marked contrast to the woman who was the trigger for Ona's escape and the reason why Philadelphia was in Georgetown in the first place: Eliza Custis Law. Surprising no one, Eliza and Thomas Law's marriage did not last. They separated in 1804, not long after Martha Washington's death, and were officially divorced in 1810. Thomas Law was granted custody of their daughter, Elizabeth. Eliza moved to a small home in Alexandria, Virginia. This was still a time when divorce was rare and a husband controlled the property within a family, even if it was technically owned by the wife. What was unclear to everyone was how the enslaved property was affected by a divorce.

Meanwhile, Philadelphia Costin had moved forward with her personal life despite the upheaval at the home of her owners. By 1807, Philadelphia and William Costin already had two children, two-year-old Louisa and four-month-old Ann. William Costin had begun his relatively prosperous work at the Bank of Washington, where for more than twenty-five years he worked as a porter. Just about everyone who knew him, white and black, respected him—including Thomas and Eliza Law.

Thomas Law, like George Washington, was undergoing a gradual change of heart about slavery. He was not an abolitionist and had lived with and profited from slave labor during his time in the United States. But he was also affected by the increasingly loud talk about black freedom. Like his grandfather-in-law

George Washington, Thomas eventually took action. On June 13, 1807, with the agreement of Eliza, Thomas Law gave Philadelphia Costin her freedom, signing her manumission papers in consideration of a one-dollar payment. Thomas Law also freed Philadelphia Costin's two children, Louisa and Ann.

Ona at this time had three young children. Technically all of them were still the property of the Custis grandchildren and would be for their entire lives.

Back in Washington, DC, William Costin was blazing his own trail of prosperity, ingenuity, and activism. He was one of the most notable members of early black society in Washington, buying property and accumulating a moderate degree of wealth over his lifetime. His free status allowed him to fight more publicly for the rights of free blacks and to help those who were still enslaved. This was important because tensions were rising everywhere over the issue of slavery—and Washington, DC's government played its own ugly role when, in 1808, it established a particularly hateful policy called the "black codes."

Black codes required that every free and enslaved black person be in their homes by ten o'clock at night. If a person broke curfew, they, or their owners, would

ERICA ARMSTRONG DUNBAR and KATHLEEN VAN CLEVE

have to pay a fine. As time passed and the free black population in the capital continued to grow, the city government decided they had to impose even more restrictions on black people. By 1812 all free blacks had to register with the government and carry a certificate of freedom with them at all times.

The worst was still to come. By 1821 the new mayor, Samuel Smallwood, had introduced a new requirement that every free black person needed to show him three letters of recommendation from white citizens that stated the free black person had good character. And then Smallwood imposed something called a "peace bond," which required free black men to pay the city twenty dollars as proof of their commitment to good behavior. This was the last straw for William Costin, who took the drastic step of *suing* the city government. In court William argued that the Constitution "knows no distinction of color."

He won his case, and the judge did not make William pay the peace bond. But he won his case only, and the peace bonds and the black codes persisted.

William decided to turn his energies elsewhere. If he couldn't fight the law and win for all black men and women, he would use the law to his advantage. He became, technically speaking, a slave owner.

Throughout the 1820s, William Costin purchased a number of enslaved men and women, many of whom had a direct connection to Mount Vernon.

And then, as soon as the legal purchase was completed, he freed them.

By the 1820s, Ona was living in poverty in the woods in New Hampshire. Jack, her husband, was dead. She had undoubtedly spent many days and nights wondering about the welfare of her family at Mount Vernon. She probably wished that her children could have met her relatives, played with their cousins, heard family folklore. It seems unfair that she never learned that her own brother-in-law had freed members of her family; that she never knew that her little sister, Philadelphia, and her sister's husband, William, were living a life as full and free and prosperous as Ona could ever have imagined.

Still, when Ona was interviewed near the end of her life, she sounded as if she were a woman wholly at peace. Maybe she sensed that change was stirring throughout the country; maybe she already believed that life would be better for her descendants. It is even possible that maybe, there in her final years, Ona Maria Judge Staines, the woman described as having a "fire that kindled in her age-bedimmed eye," understood that by seeking and claiming her own

ERICA ARMSTRONG DUNBAR and KATHLEEN VAN CLEVE

freedom from the grotesquerie that is slavery, she had propped open the door to freedom itself.

Ona led the way not only for her sister, Philadelphia Costin, but for all her enslaved brothers and sisters, step by courageous step.

GRANITE FREEMAN.

"Liberty, the Right of All: Law, Its Defence."

Vol. I.   CONCORD, N. H., THURSDAY, MAY 30, 1845.   No. 47.

PUBLISHED EVERY THURSDAY.

J. K. HOOD, Editor and Proprietor.

Office—corner of Main & Court Street, 34 doors from
No. 50 MAIN STREET.

TERMS,

$1.00 per Year in Advance.
$1.50 cents in one advance, $2.00 if not...

GRANITE FREEMAN.

Washington's Runaway Slave.

The relation of Christianity to Politics.

Apology for Pharaoh.

Execution of James Eager.

CONCORD, N.H., THURSDAY, MAY 22, 1845

Washington's Runaway Slave.

There is now living, in the borders of the town of Greenland N.H., *a runaway slave of* GEN WASHINGTON, *at present supported by the County of Rockingham.* Her name, at the time of her elopement was ONA MARIA JUDGE. She is not able to give the year of her escape but says that she came from Philadelphia, just after the close of Washington's second term of the Presidency, which must fix it somewhere in the first part of the year 1797. Being a waiting maid of Mrs. Washington, she was not exposed to any peculiar hardships. If asked why she did not remain in his service, she gives two reasons, first, that she wanted to be *free*, secondly, that she understood that after the decease of her master and mistress, she was to become the property of a granddaughter of theirs, by the name of Custis, and that she was determined never to be *her* slave.

She came on board a ship commanded by CAPT. JOHN BOLLES, and bound to Portsmouth N.H. In relating it, she added "I never told his name till after he died, a few years since, lest they should punish him for bringing me away." Had she disclosed it, he might have shared the fate of Jonathan Walker, in our own day.

Some time after she arrived at Portsmouth, she married a colored sailor, by the name of STAINES, and had a family of several children, but they, together with her husband have all been dead for several years.

Washington made two attempts to recover her. First, he sent a man by the name of Bassett to *persuade* her to return; but she resisted all the arguments he employed for this end. He told her, they would set her free when she arrived at Mount Vernon, to which she replied, "I am free now and choose to remain so."

Finding all attempts to seduce her to slavery again in this manner useless, Bassett was sent once more by Washington, with orders to bring her and *her infant child by force.* The messenger, being acquainted with GOV. LANGDON, then of Portsmouth, took up lodgings with him, and disclosed to him the object of his mission. The good old Governor, (to his honor be it spoken,) must have possessed something of the spirit of modern anti-slavery. He entertained Bassett very handsomely, and in the mean time sent word to Mrs. Staines, to leave town before twelve o'clock at night, which she did, retired to a place of concealment, and escaped the clutches of the oppressor. Shortly after this, Washington died, and, said she, "they never troubled me any more after he was gone."

Being asked how she escaped, she replied substantially as follows, "Whilst they were packing up to go to Virginia, I was packing to go, I didn't know where; for I knew that if I went back to Virginia, I never should get my liberty. I had friends among the colored people of Philadelphia, had my things carried there before hand and left while they were eating dinner."

Mrs. Staines does not know her age, but is probably not far from eighty. She is a light mulatto, so light that she might easily pass for a white woman, small of stature, and, although disabled by two successive attacks of palsy, remarkably erect and elegant in her form.

The facts here related, are known through this region, and may be relied on as substantially correct. Probably they were not for years given to the public, through fear of her recapture; but this reason no longer exists, since she is too old and infirm to be of sufficient value to repay the expense of search.

Though a houseservant she had no education, nor any valuable religious instruction; says she never heard Washington pray, and does not believe that he was accustomed to. "Mrs. Washington used to *read* prayers but I don't call that praying." Since her escape she has learned to read, trusts she has been made "wise unto salvation," and is, I think, connected with a church in Portsmouth.

When asked if she is not sorry she left Washington, as she has labored so much harder since, than before, her reply is "No, I am free, and have, I trust, been made a child of God by the means."

Never shall I forget the fire that kindled in her age-bedimmed eye, or the smile that played upon her withered countenance, as I spake of that Redeemer in whom there is neither "bond nor free," who loves his people to the end, and as I bowed with her at the mercy seat and commended her to Him "who heareth prayer" and who regards "the poor and needy when they cry," I felt that were it mine to choose, I would not exchange her possessions, "rich in faith," and sustained, while tottering over the grave, by "a hope full of immortality," for all the glory and renown of him, whose slave she was.

STRATHAM, MAY, 1845.   T.H.A.

GRANITE FREEMAN

Washington's Runaway Slave.

There is now living, in the borders of the town of Greenland N. H., *a runaway slave of* Gen. Washington, *at present supported by the County of Rockingham.* Her name, at the time of her elopement was Ona Maria Judge. She is not able to give the year of her escape but says that she came from Philadelphia, just after the close of Washington's second term of the Presidency, which must fix it somewhere in the first part of the year 1797. Being a waiting maid of Mrs. Washington, she was not exposed to any peculiar hardships. If asked why she did not remain in his service, she gives two reasons, first, that she wanted to be free, secondly, that she understood that after the decease of her master and mistress, she was to become the property of a grand-daughter of theirs, by the name of Custis, and that she was determined never to be *her* slave.

She came on board a ship commanded by Capt. John Bolles, and bound to Portsmouth N. H. In relating it, she added "I never told his name till after he died, a few years since, lest they should punish him for bringing me away." Had she disclosed it, he might have shared the fate of Jonathan Walker, in our own day.

Some time after she arrived at Portsmouth, she married a colored sailor, by the name of Staines, and had a family of several children, but they, together with her husband have all been dead for several years.

Washington made two attempts to recover her. First, he sent a man by the name of Bassett to *persuade* her to return: but she resisted all the arguments he employed for this end. He told her, they would set her free when she arrived at Mount Vernon, to which she replied, "I am free now and choose to remain so."

Finding all attempts to seduce her to slavery again in this manner useless, Bassett was sent once more by Washington, with orders to bring her and *her infant child by force.* The messenger, being acquainted with Gov. Langdon, then of Portsmouth, took up lodgings with him, and disclosed to him the object of his mission. The good old Governor, (to his honor be it spoken,) must have possessed something of the spirit of modern anti-slavery. He entertained Bassett very handsomely, and in the mean time sent word to Mrs. Staines, to leave town before twelve o'clock at night, which she did, retired to a place of concealment, and escaped the clutches of the oppressor. Shortly after this, Washington died, and, said she, "they never troubled me any more after he was gone."

Being asked how she escaped, she replied substantially as follows, "Whilst they were packing up to go to Virginia. I was packing to go, I did n't know where; for I knew that if I went back to Virginia. I never should get my liberty. I had friends among the colored people of Philadelphia, had my things carried there before hand and left while they were eating dinner."

Mrs. Staines does not know her age, but is probably not far from eighty. She is a light mulatto, so light that she might easily pass for a white woman, small of stature, and, although disabled by two successive attacks of palsy, remarkably erect and elegant in her form.

The facts here related, are known through this region, and may be relied on as substantially correct. Probably they were not for years given to the public, through fear of her recapture; but this reason no longer exists, since she is too old and infirm to be of sufficient value to repay the expense of search.

Though a house servant she had no education, nor any valuable religious instruction; says she never heard Washington pray, and does not believe that he was accustomed to. "Mrs. Washington used to *read* prayers but I do n't call that praying." Since her escape she has learned to read, trusts she has been made "wise unto salvation," and is, I think, connected with a church in Portsmouth.

When asked if she is not sorry she left Washington, as she has labored so much harder since, than before, her reply is "No, I am free, and have, I trust, been made a child of God by the means."

Never shall I forget the fire that kindled in her age-bedimmed eye, or the smile that played upon her withered countenance, as I spoke of that Redeemer in whom there is neither "bond nor free," who loves his people to the end, and as I bowed with her at the mercy seat and commended her to Him "who heareth prayer" and who regards "the poor and needy when they cry," I felt that were it mine to choose, I would not exchange her possessions, "rich in faith," and sustained, while tottering over the grave, by "a hope full of immortality," for all the glory and renown of him, whose slave she was.

Stratham, May, 1845.   T. H. A.

SELECTED BIBLIOGRAPHY

Printed and Online Primary Sources

Adams, John. John Adams to Abigail Adams, 23 February 1796 [electronic edition]. In *Adams Family Papers: An Electronic Archive.* Massachusetts Historical Society. http://www.masshist.org/digitaladams/.

Bouton, Nathaniel. *Documents and Records Relating to the Province of New-Hampshire from 1692 to 1722: Being Part II of Papers Relating to That Period; Containing the "Journal of the Council and General Assembly."* Manchester, NH: John B. Clarke, State Printer, 1869.

Brewster, Charles. "Washington and Slavery: From Mrs. Kirkland's Life of Washington." *Portsmouth Journal of Literature and Politics,* 7 March 1857.

Crackel, Theodore, ed. *The Papers of George Washington Digital Edition.* Charlottesville: University of Virginia Press, Rotunda, 2007–.

Description of a Slave Ship. London, 1789. Rare Books and Special Collections, Princeton University Library. https://blogs.princeton.edu/rarebooks/2008/05/219-years-ago-description-of-a/.

Elizabeth Van Lew Album 1845–1897. Manuscripts Collection at the Virginia Historical Society.

"Examination Days: The New York African Free School Collection." New-York Historical Society. https://www.nyhistory.org/web/africanfreeschool/#.

George Washington Papers 1741–1799: Series 4. General Correspondence. 1697–1799. The Library of Congress, Washington, DC.

Lear, Tobias. Tobias Lear to George Augustine Washington, 3 May 1789. George Washington Manuscript Collection. Book, Manuscript, and Special Collections Library, Duke University.

Lewis, Robert. "Journal of a Journey from Fredericksburg, Virginia to New York, May 13–20, 1789." Digital Collections from George Washington's Mount Vernon.

"Madison Debates September 17."Yale Law School Avalon Project. http:// avalon.law.yale.edu/18th_century/debates_917.asp.

New Hampshire Vital Statistics, Concord, NH. Ancestry.com. *New Hampshire, Death and Burial Records Index, 1654-1949* [database online]. Provo, UT: Ancestry.com Operations, Inc., 2011.

Peter Family Archives, Fred W. Smith National Library for the Study of George Washington at Mount Vernon.

Quarterly Abstracts of Seamen's Protection Certificates, New York City, NY 1815– 1869. National Archives and Records Administration. Washington, DC. Ancestry.com. *U.S., Seamen's Protection Certificates, 1792–1869* [database online]. Provo, UT: Ancestry.com Operations, Inc., 2010.

Records of the Government of the District of Columbia. Record Group 351. National Archives, Washington, DC.

Seaman's Protection Certificates for Portland, ME. National Archives, Washington, DC.

Thomas Law Family Papers. Collections of the Maryland Historical Society.

Town Records of Greenland, New Hampshire, 1750–1851. Greenland Town Vault, Town Hall, Greenland, New Hampshire.

The Washington Family Papers. Collections at the Library of Congress.

Washington, George. George Washington to Oliver Wolcott, 1 September 1796. Collections of the Connecticut Historical Society.

———. *The Diary of George Washington, from the first day of October 1789 to the tenth day of March, 1790.* New York: New York Public Library. https://archive.org/details/diarywashington00lossgoog.

———. *The Papers of George Washington.* Vol. 2, *April–June 1789.* Edited by W. W. Abbott. Charlottesville: University of Virginia Press, 1987.

Washington, Martha. Martha Washington to Frances B. Washington, 8 June 1789. Gilder Lehrman Institute of American History. http://www .gilderlehrman.org/collections/treasures-from-the-collection /martha-washington-first-lady's-grandchildren-were-her-top-.

———. Martha Washington to Fanny Bassett Washington, 23 October 1789, in Martha Washington. http://www.marthawashington.us /items/show/25.

Weld, Isaac Jr. *Travels through the states of North America and the provinces of Upper and Lower Canada during the years 1795, 1796, and 1797.* London, 1799.

Newspapers

Argus, or Greenleaf's New Daily Advertiser (New York, NY)

Claypoole's American Daily Advertiser (Philadelphia, PA)

Daily National Intelligencer (Washington, DC)

Exeter News-Letter (Portsmouth, NH)

Finlay's American Naval and Commercial Register (Philadelphia)

Granite Freeman (Concord, NH)

Liberator (Boston, MA)

Minerva (New York, NY)

New-Hampshire Gazette (Portsmouth, NH)

New York Journal (New York, NY)

Oracle of the Day (Portsmouth, NH)

Pennsylvania Freeman (Philadelphia)

Pennsylvania Gazette (Philadelphia)

Philadelphia (PA) Gazette (Federal Gazette)

Portsmouth (NH) Journal

Published Secondary Sources

Adams, Catherine, and Elizabeth H. Pleck. *Love of Freedom: Black Women in Colonial and Revolutionary New England.* Oxford: Oxford University Press, 2010.

Alexander, Leslie M. *African or American?: Black Identity and Political Activism in New York City, 1784–1861.* Urbana: University of Illinois Press, 2008.

Baker, William Spohn. *Washington after the Revolution; 1784–1799.* Philadelphia: n.p., 1897.

Barratt, Carrie Rebora, Gilbert Stuart, and Ellen Gross Miles. *Gilbert Stuart.* New York: Metropolitan Museum of Art, 2004.

Berlin, Ira. *Many Thousands Gone: The First Two Centuries of Slavery in North America.* Cambridge: Harvard University Press, 2000.

Berry, Daina Ramey. *"Swing the Sickle for the Harvest Is Ripe": Gender and Slavery in Antebellum Georgia.* Urbana: University of Illinois Press, 2007.

Blanton, Wyndham. "Washington's Medical Knowledge and Its Sources." *Annals of Medical History* 4.932 (1932): 52–61. Web.

Blassingame, John W. *The Slave Community: Plantation Life in the Antebellum South.* New York: Oxford University Press, 1972.

Block, Sharon. *Rape and Sexual Power in Early America.* Chapel Hill: The University of North Carolina Press, 2006.

Blockson, Charles L. "Patriot, White House Steward and Restaurateur Par Excellence." 20 November 2014. http://library.temple.edu /collections/blockson/fraunces. Web.

Bolster, W. Jeffrey. *Black Jacks: African American Seamen in the Age of Sail.* Cambridge, MA: Harvard University Press, 1997.

Brady, Patricia. *Martha Washington: An American Life.* New York: Viking, 2005.

Brighton, Ray. *The Checkered Career of Tobias Lear.* Portsmouth, NH: Portsmouth Marine Society, 1985.

Brookhiser, Richard. *James Madison.* New York: Basic, 2011.

Brown, Letitia Woods. *Free Negroes in the District of Columbia, 1790–1846.* New York: Oxford University Press, 1972.

Brown, Letitia Woods. "Residence Patterns of Negroes in the District of Columbia, 1800–1860." In *Records of the Columbia Historical Society.* Vol. 47. Washington, DC: Columbia Historical Society, 1971.

Brown, Warren. *History of the Town of Hampton Falls, New Hampshire: From the Time of the First Settlement Within Its Borders, 1640 until 1900.* Manchester, NH: John B. Clarke, 1900.

Bryan, Helen. *Martha Washington: First Lady of Liberty.* New Jersey: Wiley, 2002.

Callcott, Margaret Law. *Mistress of Riversdale: The Plantation Letters of Rosalie Stier Calvert.* Baltimore: Johns Hopkins, 1992.

Camp, Stephanie M. H. *Closer to Freedom: Enslaved Women and Everyday Resistance in the Plantation South.* Chapel Hill: The University of North Carolina Press, 2004.

Carretta, Vincent. *Phillis Wheatley: Biography of a Genius in Bondage.* Athens, GA: University of Georgia Press, 2011.

Chernow, Ron. *Washington: A Life.* New York: Penguin, 2010.

Clark, Christopher. *The Roots of Rural Capitalism: Western Massachusetts, 1780–1860.* Ithaca: Cornell University Press, 1990.

Craft, William, and Ellen Craft. *Running a Thousand Miles for Freedom.* New York: Arno, 1969.

Crosby, Molly Caldwell. *The American Plague: The Untold Story of Yellow Fever, the Epidemic That Shaped Our History.* New York: Berkley, 2006.

Cunningham, Valerie. "The First Blacks of Portsmouth." *Historical New Hampshire* 41, no. 4 (Winter 1989). Web.

Dabel, Jane E. *A Respectable Woman: The Public Roles of African American Women in 19th-Century New York.* New York: New York University Press, 2008.

Decatur, Stephen, and Tobias Lear. *Private Affairs of George Washington, from the Records and Accounts of Tobias Lear, Esquire, His Secretary.* Boston: Houghton Mifflin, 1933.

Douglass, William. *Annals of the First African Church, in the United States of America Now Styled the African Episcopal Church of St. Thomas, Philadelphia, in Its Connection with the Early Struggles of the Colored People to Improve Their Condition, with the Co-operation of the Friends, and Other Philanthropists; Partly Derived from the Minutes of a Beneficial Society, Established by Absalom Jones, Richard Allen and Others, in 1787, and Partly from the Minutes of the Aforesaid Church.* Philadelphia: King & Baird, Printers, 1862.

Dunbar, Erica Armstrong. *A Fragile Freedom: African American Women and Emancipation in the Antebellum City.* New Haven: Yale University Press, 2008.

Egerton, Douglas R. *Death or Liberty: African Americans and Revolutionary America.* Oxford: Oxford University Press, 2009.

———. *Gabriel's Rebellion: The Virginia Slave Conspiracies of 1800 and 1802.* Chapel Hill: The University of North Carolina Press, 1993.

———. *He Shall Go Out Free: The Lives of Denmark Vesey.* Lanham, MD: Rowman & Littlefield, 2004.

Ellis, Joseph J. *American Creation: Triumphs and Tragedies at the Founding of the Republic.* New York: Alfred A. Knopf, 2007.

Fields, Joseph E. *Worthy Partner: The Papers of Martha Washington.* Westport, CT: Greenwood, 1994.

Finkelman, Paul. *Slavery and the Founders: Race and Liberty in the Age of Jefferson.* Armonk, NY: M. E. Sharpe, 1996.

First Census of the United States, 1790: Records of the State Enumerations, 1782 to 1785: Virginia. Spartanburg, SC: Reprint, 1974.

Fitzpatrick, John C. *The Writings of George Washington: From the Original Manuscript Sources 1745–1799.* Washington, DC: United States Government Printing Office, 1931.

Flexner, James Thomas. *George Washington.* Boston: Little, Brown, 1972.

"Founders Online: Washington's Slave List, June 1799." *Washington's Slave List, June 1799.* 15 June 2015. http://founders.archives.gov/documents /Washington/06-04-02-0405.

Freeman, Douglas Southall. *George Washington: A Biography.* 7 vols. New York: Charles Scribner's Sons, 1948–57. Volume 7 completed by John A. Caroll and Mary Wells Ashworth.

Furstenburg, Francois. *In the Name of the Father: Washington's Legacy, Slavery, and the Making of a Nation.* New York: Penguin Books, 2006.

Galenson, David W. "The Rise and Fall of Indentured Servitude in the Americas: An Economic Analysis." *The Journal of Economic History* 44.01 (1984): 1. Web.

Gerson, Evelyn B. "A Thirst for Complete Freedom: Why Fugitive Slave Ona Judge Staines Never Returned to Her Master, President George Washington." Thesis. Harvard University.

Girard, Philippe R. *The Slaves Who Defeated Napoleon: Toussaint Louverture and the Haitian War of Independence, 1801–1804.* Tuscaloosa: The University of Alabama Press, 2011.

Gordon-Reed, Annette. *The Hemingses of Monticello: An American Family.* New York: W. W. Norton, 2009.

Grizzard, Frank E. *George Washington: A Biographical Companion.* Santa Barbara, CA: ABC-CLIO, 2002.

Harris, Leslie M. *In the Shadow of Slavery: African Americans in New York City, 1626–1863.* Chicago: University of Chicago Press, 2003.

Harvey, Tamara, and Greg O'Brien, eds. *George Washington's South.* Gainesville: University Press of Florida, 2004.

Heads of Families at the First Census of the United States, Taken in the Year 1790: New Hampshire. Spartanburg, SC: Reprint, 1964.

Heads of Families at the First Census of the United States Taken in the Year 1790; Records of the State Enumerations: 1782–1785, Virginia. Baltimore: Genealogical Pub., 1970.

Herbert, Catherine A. "The French Element in Pennsylvania in the 1790s: The Francophone Immigrants' Impact." *Pennsylvania Magazine of History and Biography* 108 (1984): 451–70. Web.

Hirschfeld, Fritz. *George Washington and Slavery: A Documentary Portrayal.* Columbia: University of Missouri, 1997.

Hodges, Graham Russell. *Root & Branch: African Americans in New York and East Jersey, 1613–1863.* Chapel Hill: The University of North Carolina Press, 1999.

Hoffman, Henry B. "President Washington's Cherry Street Residence." *The New York Historical Society Quarterly Bulletin* 23 (1939): 90–103.

Hunter, Tera W. *To 'Joy My Freedom: Southern Black Women's Lives and Labors after the Civil War.* Cambridge, MA: Harvard University Press, 1997.

Jacobs, Harriet A., John S. Jacobs, and Jean Fagan Yellin. *Incidents in the Life of a Slave Girl: Written by Herself, Now with "A True Tale of Slavery" by John S. Jacobs.* Cambridge, MA: Belknap, 2009.

Jones, Jacqueline. *Labor of Love, Labor of Sorrow: Black Women, Work, and the Family from Slavery to the Present.* New York: Basic, 1985.

Kaminski, John P., and Jill Adair McCaughan. *A Great and Good Man: George Washington in the Eyes of His Contemporaries.* Madison, WI: Madison House, 1989.

Kelly, Catherine E. *In the New England Fashion: Reshaping Women's Lives in the Nineteenth Century.* Ithaca, NY: Cornell University Press, 1999.

Kirkland, Caroline M. *Memoirs of Washington.* New York: D. Appleton, 1857.

Klepp, Susan. "Seasoning and Society: Racial Differences in Mortality in Eighteenth-Century Philadelphia." *William and Mary Quarterly* 51 (1994): 473–506. Web.

Knox, J. H. Mason, Jr. "The Medical History of George Washington, His Physicians, Friends, and Advisers." *Bulletin of the Institute of the History of Medicine* 1 (1933): 174–91. Web.

Lawler, Edward, Jr. "The President's House in Philadelphia: The Rediscovery of a Lost Landmark." *Pennsylvania Magazine of History and Biography* 126, no.1 (2002): 5–95. Web.

Lossing, Benson John. *Martha Washington.* New York: J. C. Buttre, 1865.

Lyons, Clare A. *Sex among the Rabble: An Intimate History of Gender & Power in the Age of Revolution, Philadelphia, 1730–1830.* Chapel Hill: Published for the Omohundro Institute of Early American History and Culture, Williamsburg, Virginia, by the University of North Carolina Press, 2006.

Married Women and the Law. Coverture in England and the Common Law World. Montreal: McGill-Queen's University Press, 2013.

Matthaei, Julie A. *An Economic History of Women in America: Women's Work, the Sexual Division of Labor, and the Development of Capitalism.* New York: Schocken, 1982.

McCullough, David G. *John Adams.* New York: Simon & Schuster, 2001.

McHenry, Elizabeth. *Forgotten Readers: Recovering the Lost History of African American Literary Societies.* Durham: Duke University Press, 2002.

McManus, Edgar J. *Black Bondage in the North.* Syracuse, NY: Syracuse University Press, 1973.

Melish, Joanne Pope. *Disowning Slavery: Gradual Emancipation and "Race" in New England, 1780–1860.* Ithaca: Cornell University Press, 1998.

Moore, Lindsay. "Women and Property Litigation in Seventeenth-Century England and North America." In *Married Women and the Law: Coverture in England and the Common Law World,* edited by Tim Stretton and K. J. Kesselring. Canada: McGill-Queen's University Press, 2013.

Morgan, Jennifer L. *Laboring Women: Reproduction and Gender in New World Slavery.* Philadelphia: University of Pennsylvania Press, 2004.

Morgan, Philip D., and Michael L. Nicholls. "Slave Flight: Mount Vernon, Virginia, and the Wider Atlantic World." In *George Washington's South,* edited by Tamara Harvey and Greg O'Brien, 199–222. Gainesville: University Press of Florida, 2004.

Morgan, Philip. "'To Get Quit of Negroes': George Washington and Slavery." *Journal of American Studies* 39.3 (2005): 403–29. Web.

Nash, Gary B., and Jean R. Soderlund. *Freedom by Degrees: Emancipation in Pennsylvania and Its Aftermath.* New York: Oxford University Press, 1991.

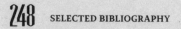

———. *First City: Philadelphia and the Forging of Historical Memory.* Philadelphia: University of Pennsylvania Press, 2002.

———. *Forging Freedom: The Formation of Philadelphia's Black Community, 1720–1840.* Cambridge, MA: Harvard University Press, 1900.

———. *The Forgotten Fifth: African Americans in the Age of Revolution.* Cambridge, MA: Harvard University Press, 2006.

Nelson, Charles B. *History of Stratham, New Hampshire, 1631–1900.* Somers-worth, NH: New Hampshire Publishing Company, 1965.

Newman, Richard S. *Freedom's Prophet: Bishop Richard Allen, the AME Church, and the Black Founding Fathers.* New York: New York University Press, 2008.

Ohline, Howard A. "Slavery, Economics, and Congressional Politics." In *Establishing the New Regime: The Washington Administration,* edited by Peter Onuf. New York: Routledge, 1991. 335–60.

"Our House? The President's House at Independence National Historical Park." *The Pennsylvania Magazine of History and Biography* 135.2 (2011): 191–97.

Pawley, Christine. *Reading Places: Literacy, Democracy, and the Public Library in Cold War America.* Amherst: University of Massachusetts Press, 2010.

"Philadelphia Household Account Book, 1793–1797." *Pennsylvania Magazine of History and Biography* 30.3 (1906): 47–48. Web.

Piersen, William Dillon. *Black Yankees: The Development of an Afro-American Subculture in Eighteenth-Century New England.* Amherst: University of Massachusetts Press, 1988.

Powell, J. H. *Bring Out Your Dead; the Great Plague of Yellow Fever in Philadelphia in 1793.* Edited by J. Kenneth Foster, Mary F. Jenkins, and Anna Coxe Toogood. Philadelphia: University of Pennsylvania Press, 1949.

Prussing, Eugene Ernst. *The Estate of George Washington, Deceased.* Boston: Little, Brown, 1927.

Puckett, Newbell Niles, and Murray Heller. *Black Names in America: Origins and Usage.* Boston: G. K. Hall, 1975.

Quarles, Benjamin. *The Negro in the Making of America.* New York: Collier, 1969.

Ribblett, David L. *Nelly Custis: Child of Mount Vernon.* Mount Vernon, VA: Mount Vernon Ladies' Association, 1993.

Rice, Kym. *A Documentary History of Fraunces Tavern: The 18th Century*. New York: Fraunces Tavern Museum, 1985.

Riley, Edward M. "Philadelphia, The Nation's Capital, 1790–1800." *Pennsylvania History* 20.4 (1953): 357–79. Web.

Rogers, Helen Hoban. *Freedom & Slavery Documents in the District of Columbia*. Baltimore: Published for the Author by Gateway, 2007.

Rothman, Adam. *Slave Country: American Expansion and the Origins of the Deep South*. Cambridge, MA: Harvard University Press, 2005.

Sammons, Mark J., and Valerie Cunningham. *Black Portsmouth: Three Centuries of African-American Heritage*. Durham: University of New Hampshire Press, 2004.

Sawyer, Roland D. "New Hampshire Pioneers of Religious Liberty: Rev. Elias Smith of Portsmouth, New Hampshire's Theodore Parker." In *The Granite Monthly: A New Hampshire Magazine Devoted to History, Biography, and State Progress*. Concord, NH, 1918.

Schwartz, Marie Jenkins. *Born in Bondage: Growing up Enslaved in the Antebellum South*. Cambridge, MA: Harvard University Press, 2000.

Schwartz, Philip J., ed. *Slavery at the Home of George Washington*. Mount Vernon, VA: The Mount Vernon Ladies' Association, 2001.

Smith, Billy, and Richard Wojtowicz. *Blacks Who Stole Themselves: Advertisements for Runaways in the Pennsylvania Gazette, 1728–1790*. Philadelphia: University of Pennsylvania Press, 1989.

Smith, Billy G. *The "Lower Sort": Philadelphia's Laboring People, 1750–1800*. Ithaca, NY: Cornell University Press, 1990.

Thane, Elswyth. *Mount Vernon Family*. New York: Crowell-Collier, 1968.

Thompson, Mary V. "Control and Resistance: A Study of George Washington and Slavery." The Historical Society of Western Pennsylvania. Oct. 2000. Lecture.

Ulrich, Laurel Thatcher. *The Age of Homespun: Objects and Stories in the Creation of an American Myth*. New York: Knopf, 2001.

———. *A Midwife's Tale: The Life of Martha Ballard, Based on Her Diary, 1785–1812*. New York: Knopf, 1990.

United States. *Proceedings and Debates of the House of Representatives of the United States at the Second Session of the Second Congress, Begun at the City of Philadelphia, November 5, 1792*. "Annals of Congress, 2nd

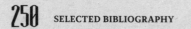

Congress, 2nd Session (November 5, 1792 to March 2, 1793)," 2nd Cong., 2nd sess. Cong. Rept., 1414–15. Web. Mar. 2014. http://memory.loc.gov/cgi-bin/ampage?collId=llac&fileName=003/llac003.db&recNum=702.

Waldstreicher, David. *Runaway America: Benjamin Franklin, Slavery, and the American Revolution.* New York: Hill and Wang, 2004.

———. "The Wheatleyan Moment." *Early American Studies: An Interdisciplinary Journal* 9.3 (2011): 522–51. Web.

Washington, George. *The Diaries of George Washington.* Edited by Donald Jackson and Dorothy Twohig. Vol. 6. Charlottesville: University of Virginia Press, 1976.

———. *George Washington's Diaries: An Abridgement.* Edited by Dorothy Twohig. Charlottesville: University of Virginia Press, 1999.

"Washington's Household Account Book 1793–1797." *Pennsylvania Magazine of History and Biography* 31 (1907): 142. Web.

Weld, Isaac. *Travels through the States of North America and the Provinces of Upper and Lower Canada during the Years 1795, 1796, and 1797.* London: Printed for John Stockdale, 1799.

Wharton, Anne H. "Washington's New York Residence in 1789." *Lippincott's Monthly Magazine* 43 (1889): 741–45. Web.

Whipple, Blaine. *History and Genealogy of "Elder" John Whipple of Ipswich, Massachusetts: His English Ancestors and American Descendants.* Victoria, BC: Trafford, 2003.

White, Ashli. *Encountering Revolution: Haiti and the Making of the Early Republic.* Baltimore: Johns Hopkins University Press, 2010.

White, Deborah G. *Ar'n't I a Woman?: Female Slaves in the Plantation South.* New York: W. W. Norton, 1985.

White, Shane. *Somewhat More Independent: The End of Slavery in New York City, 1770–1810.* Athens: University of Georgia Press, 1991.

Whitman, T. Stephen. *The Price of Freedom: Slavery and Manumission in Baltimore and Early National Maryland.* Lexington, KY: University Press of Kentucky, 1997.

Wiencek, Henry. *An Imperfect God: George Washington, His Slaves, and the Creation of America.* New York: Farrar, Straus and Giroux, 2003.

Williams, Heather Andrea. *Self-Taught: African American Education in Slavery and Freedom.* Chapel Hill: The University of North Carolina Press, 2005.

Wong, Edlie L. *Neither Fugitive nor Free: Atlantic Slavery, Freedom Suits, and the Legal Culture of Travel.* New York: New York University Press, 2009.

Wood, Betty. *Slavery in Colonial America, 1619–1776.* Lanham, MD: Rowman & Littlefield, 2005.

Wood, Gordon S. *Revolutionary Characters: What Made the Founders Different.* New York: Penguin Books, 2007.